THE GOLDMINE OF YOUR MIND

(Your Fast Track to Abundance)

FIND PURPOSE, BOOST UP YOUR POSITIVITY, AND ACHIEVE FUNCTIONAL SUCCESS WITH THE POWER OF YOUR MIND

AYO BENSON OLAREWAJU

Publisher's note
Every possible effort has been made to ensure that the information contained in the book is accurate at the time of going to press, and the publishers and the author cannot accept responsibility for any errors or omissions, however caused. No responsibility for loss or damage occasioned to any person acting, or refraining from action, as a result of the material in this publication can be accepted by the editor, the publishers or the editor.

First published in Great Britain in 2015 under the title: ***The Goldmine of Your Mind (Your Fast Track to Abundance)***
Apart from any fair dealings for the purposes of research or private study, or criticism or review, as permitted under the Copyright, Designs and Patents Acts 1988, this publication can only be reproduced, stored, or transmitted, in any form or by means, with the prior permission in writing to the publisher, or in any case of reprographic reproduction in accordance with the terms and licences issued by the CLA. Enquiries concerning reproduction outside this terms should be sent to the publishers:
Mannabooks Inc.

© **Ayo Benson Olarewaju, 2015**
The right of Ayo Benson Olarewaju to be identified as the author of this work has been asserted in accordance with the Copyrights, Designs, and Patents Acts 1988.

British Library Cataloguing in Publication Data
A CIP record for this book is available from the British Library
ISBN   978-0-9934939-0-4

Typeset/Design by **Xandy Daehnhardt**
Editorial/Publishing Consultant **– Segun Martins Fajemisin**
(infomediaworks ltd)

Dedication

This book is dedicated to the memory of my loving sister Mojisola Olarewaju who was murdered in a contrived armed robbery by greedy people for her money! You will remain in our thoughts forever. My major motivation for writing this book is to keep your memory alive; I know you are very proud looking down from heaven!

You will remain in our memory forever!

Endorsements for:
The Goldmine of your Mind (Your Fast Track to Abundance)

This book addresses the power of the mind and how valuable it is to reach the depth of our minds. The book also looks into, and encourages people to be successful entrepreneurs by using the power of their minds to cultivate the habit of positive thoughts. I will encourage people to buy and read the book because it is a powerhouse of knowledge that can help them to unlock their inner power to achieve success.

Cllr Adedamola Aminu
Former Mayor of Lambeth 2014-15
President Association of Nigerian Academics UK

Think out of the box, think extraordinarily and deeply, and all the latent potentials will be brought to fore. Having done this, use every ethical opportunity to apply such potentials to be a successful person. This is the message of this book authored by a successful Chartered Accountant. The message is worth embracing.

Doyin Owolabi BSc (Econs), MILR, FNIM, FCA
(Past President, Institute of Chartered Accountants of Nigeria)

"An inspiring read, Ayo Benson's book appeals to people across the age, status, professional and socio-cultural divides. Written from a business perspective, this tome has all the elements to instil in the discerning reader those transferable skills that may engender success in any chosen field of human endeavour. It is an insightful and well-written book.

Identifying one's area of strength, revving up the zeal to achieve life's objectives and pushing that extra hard for accomplishment are instructive to the attainment of success. *The Goldmine of Your Mind (Your Fast Track to Abundance)* outlines the requisite steps to follow in simple, everyday language. It challenges as forcefully as it entreats the reader to take charge of their destinies. It is a motivational book of a rare kind, an agile methodology and a must read for all progress minded people.
Emmanuel Ojo Ademola - Professor and CM subject matter Expert. Trademark owner of (Power-Age Management Consulting) United Kingdom

Acknowledgement

I would like to thank so many people who have made this book possible. Glory be to God for his mercies which endure forever. Thanks to my dad John Omotayo Olarewaju and my mum Oreoluwa Olarewaju; I wouldn't be in a position to write a book without their love; more importantly the values and education I received. I would also acknowledge the inspirations provided by my family especially my lovely children Ayo David, Kemi Gloria and Jennifer Bolanle; I tried to do more for the world so that these kids and other kids may have a better life than our own generation.

I have to thank my good childhood friend and brother Segun Martins Fajemisin, a renowned journalist and publisher of great repute for dissecting every part of the manuscript. Segun was a source of constant encouragement throughout the process of this project and the quality of this work was greatly enhanced by his erudite contributions. I would also thank Uche Nnene a Fellow Chartered Accountant and a great friend for reading the manuscript several times over and for her contributions and encouragement to see the project through successfully. I would also like to thank Florence Kanikwu for the management of my other businesses while I was writing this book; she is a gem of a friend!

I would also thank Mr. Doyin Owolabi FCA (Past President of Institute of Chartered Accountants of

Nigeria) for his encouragement and support for this project. Dr. Sola Olarewaju is my dear brother who looks after my medical needs and a great support despite his tight schedule; I say a big thank you. My sister Lola Olarewaju for being a supportive sister at all times.

I would also acknowledge some great men whose ideas I admire through their public speaking and their books too many to mention. Some of these men were mentioned in the book for their quotes which also enhanced readers understanding of the good ideas in this book. I have to thank the celebrities as well as mere mortals whose stories, news or accomplishments were mentioned in the book to provide the right kind of flavour and motivation for the readers of this book.

Finally, I want to thank listeners of my radio program 'Goldmine of Your Mind' for their feedback and their enthusiasm to learn which ultimately led to the decision to write this book. I would like to thank some of my staff who have contributed directly or indirectly to making this piece of work a reality.

CONTENTS

Endorsements for The Goldmine of Your Mind 4
Acknowledgement 6
Preface 10

CHAPTER 1: 12
The Mind is Everything!

CHAPTER 2: 19
The Power of Thought

CHAPTER 3: 29
The Learning Machine

CHAPTER 4: 41
Finding Your Talent

CHAPTER 5: 52
Generating ideas for a new business

CHAPTER 6: 68
How to raise money for your new business

CHAPTER 7: 90
Business Environment

CHAPTER 8: 91
Branding

CHAPTER 9: 107
Procrastination: The Killer of Dreams

CHAPTER 10: 115
The Lessons of Momentum

CHAPTER 11: 122
PEOPLE: The Pillar of Progress

CHAPTER 12: 128
The Art of Selling

CHAPTER 13: 162
Conquer fear!

CHAPTER 14: 167
Communication

CHAPTER 15: 174
Negotiation

CHAPTER 16: 190
Systems, Policies and Procedures

CHAPTER 17: 197
Leadership

CHAPTER 18: 209
The Question of Money and your Belief System

CHAPTER 19: 219
Time

CHAPTER 20: 231
Mental and Physical Energy

CHAPTER 21: 238
Change: The Opportunity to Grow

CHAPTER 22: 244
Contribution

CHAPTER 23: 252
The Gift of Crisis

CHAPTER 24: 263
Goal Setting

CHAPTER 25: 268
Confidence

CHAPTER 26: 275
Determination

CHAPTER 27: 281
The End is the Beginning

ABOUT THE AUTHOR 290

Preface

The world has changed, the opportunities have expanded but there are still many people living well below the standard commensurate with the opportunities all around them. This book attempts to expand the reader's mind to see the world in a way that helps them achieve transformation for a better life.

The era of job for life is almost non-existent today and people at a time in their lives may encounter a situation where they have to make a living on their own initiatives. Few books address the issue of personal growth with an entrepreneurship accent like this one! The author being an entrepreneur realised that most business books in the market are bland and tedious without consideration for inspiring the readers to actually implement what they are learning. After decades of first-hand experience in business, he decides to put together a book that would not only teach innovative, tried and tested methods but also inspire people to apply and adapt the knowledge to succeed at anything they do in or out of business.

The content of each chapter could be used independently of previous or subsequent chapters depending on the need of the reader; however the flow from one chapter to the other is seamless and continuous. The book also addresses some of the typical skills required by entrepreneurs as well as how to deal with the inevitable challenges of business and life; where academic concepts or models are used, they are simplified for easy read.

This book is written in a popular conversational style to make it accessible to a lot of people not only to learn but to enjoy. There are a lot of personal stories of the author's experience and observations of the contemporary culture which gives the book such a stimulating flavour; there is an element of compelling readability about it.

Look for the message in this book that resonates with your current situation, study it and pick out the lessons relevant to you. This is certainly not enough; you must take actions immediately because according to Albert Einstein 'Nothing happens until something moves'! So read this book, study it, more importantly —take action!

Your Mind is a Goldmine – use it!

Uche Nnene FCCA ACA MBA PMP
Ciber UK

CHAPTER 1

The Mind is Everything!

"Great minds have purposes; others have wishes"
- Washington Irving (1783 – 1859, American author, essayist, biographer, historian, and diplomat of the early 19th century)

The title of this book could as well be *'The Dungeon of Your Mind'* and it would still have been appropriate but I choose *'The Goldmine of Your Mind'* to reflect on how useful and powerful your mind is. The other title is equally as true because that's how dangerous and powerful your mind is!

The meaning of the title is obvious enough but for the sake of clarity, I would briefly address the rationale for the title. My original thought was to allow the readers to figure out the meaning as they read this book but on second thought, I feel it is more appropriate to lay it out there to help people understand the context of the title and the content of this book as a result.

I hope the meaning does more for you than just

identify the title of this book. My observation of the world is that people place unbelievable value on resources; it is the easy excuse not to do something we know we should do. Resources are our scapegoat, it is to blame if we don't achieve or we don't meet our target or we do not pass the exam. You get the idea, the list is endless. My observation is that there is more treasure in the depth of human mind, than we can ever find under the ground. Everyone has got it, but not everyone uses it! *Goldmine of your mind* suggests that there is unlimited treasure deep in your mind and you can uncover it. The only condition is that, you must really desire it for you to reach it. This book addresses in part the fact about how valuable your mind is and how to reach the depth of your mind where you can access the enormous power readily available to you. What is the relationship between your mind, your emotions and your thoughts? Without going into the intricate details of how the brain works, the simple steps you need to understand is that your thoughts are very powerful enough to generate your emotions and in turn your emotions may dictate the direction of your life from physiological, psychological and esoteric perspectives. There is more to life and the universe than meets the eyes literally. You are most likely familiar with the phrase *'seeing is believing.'* This is a very simplistic way of looking at the world. There are so many unseen powers influencing our lives daily and whether we recognise it or not, whether we believe it or not, these unseen powers affect our lives. Some of us are connected to the unseen powers in ways we cannot even explain, and the fact that not everyone does experience it doesn't mean it does not exist. Everyone has gifts whether they recognise it or not. May I even go a step further and say whether they do use it or not!

Are you talented as an individual? If you answer yes to that question, you are right; if you answer no to that same question, you are also right! It's all a matter of belief. This is not a book on religion but once in a while, when there is compelling evidence from religion that supports the message in this book, then I would use it. We don't all have the same talent or to the same degree and the parable of Jesus about talent is quite supportive of that fact. People have varying degree of talent but it is important that you access that which you have identified and use it.

How do you uncover your talent? It is never too late to grow that talent of yours such that it provides for you the kind of life you want and the opportunity to contribute to the society.

What is the relationship between the mind and talent? Your mind is the bedrock of your talent and that's why the focus of this book is to show you how the mind works and how to access the enormous powers you could derive from using it. How the mind works is not terribly important but it helps to have an idea. The important part is to know how to use it to achieve your dream(s) whatever they are.

Talent is nothing more than an individual stumbling

on something they love to do and then focus on developing it further by doing it over and over again.

One of the questions that bother humanity and would continue to do so is why there is so much inequality in the world. Have you ever pondered the question as to why some people seem to have everything and others struggle in every area of life? I have always been searching for answers to this question for as long as I can remember in my mind as well as reading books that address the issue directly or indirectly. The truth is usually obvious and simple which is the reason why people see it but cannot recognise it. Have I found the truth about this question bothering humanity since the dawn of time or not? I heard the voice that tells me that whatever you have found so far is the truth right now so share it with the world. So here I am doing exactly what I was instructed to share and I hope it helps in a little or big way for those who accept and use it.

How does it all work? There is a sophisticated linkage between every part of the human body. I have an interesting example to tell you, I am a football follower (not a fanatic) and I am telling you so that you will understand why I picked out this example. What is the relationship between gap tooth and chronic back pain? 'Nothing' should be your answer and so is mine! David Beckham was on loan at AC Milan in his active playing days, complains about this back pain that would not go away and as an athlete it could really be difficult! To cut a long story short, the renowned Milan clinic discovers there is a linkage between his gap tooth and back pain so the solution is to close the gap tooth. Bingo, back pain disappears! How preposterous is that? You may ask a valid question that how did they discover that? Well, I have no idea - they are the experts but the lesson for me is that our body is a sophisticated and complex machine that thousands of years of study since civilisation have not wholly unravelled and that we are still trying to understand it.

May I say that thousands of years to come we would still be trying to understand it! We would never completely understand everything about this body of ours and the more we look the more things we find! So that's our body but we are supposed to be talking about mind! Okay then, the reason is that you cannot have a mind without a body, and more importantly as every part of the body is linked intricately, so is the mind linked to the body! This brings to the fore another phrase that I trust you would be familiar with: "*A sound body is a sound mind*".

Our body is critical to our existence and so is the mind. How much attention have we given to the study of the mind? Not much, I have spent significant part of my life in education and I was taught a lot of stuffs about how the body works and how to keep it prim and proper. However, not so much was said about the mind! My observation is that this is why some very bright students sometimes struggle in life just as well as the not-so-bright ones! I am very eager to launch into my findings and how it could be of help to you in your life, in your business and your relationships.

As an entrepreneur, I have realised that there are many challenges in business, but the usual business books proffer solutions which most times don't work! The fact counts that those business books are written by people who haven't done a day of business in their lives. They are thinkers and teachers no doubt and are probably fairly established in doing that for a living. There is nothing wrong with that except that the business books I have read by some entrepreneurs are much more useful to me in my business than those by professors. When I decided to write this book, I thought that I am going to share my experience and thoughts of other entrepreneurs which would not only be extremely useful to other entrepreneurs or aspiring entrepreneurs but also to people of all ages and backgrounds because the principles and ideas could be applied to any area of life and it would still work.

In business as in life, the state of mind is critical because if you don't get your mind right it would be an uphill task succeeding in business or any other endeavour of life. I have experienced this first-hand myself and I wish I could have access to a book like this when I was 18; I could easily have avoided some of my mistakes! I am a workaholic by nature because I was taught as a child that it is the way to succeed and I believed it. Is it true or not? Not really! I have seen many people work so hard in life with absolutely nothing to show for it and there are those who are in abundance with less work! The luck factor is nothing other than the universe responding to a state of mind which attracts fortunes. How do you develop such state of mind? There are so many resources with contradictory principles but the one I have found to have worked very well for me is shared at some point in this book and I hope when you discover it, you will also use it.

So this is not a book on how the mind works and it isn't a book on how to succeed in business and in life only; my goal is to write a book where I share my observation of the world and the thoughts of great men with good values; in the process, I hope you pick up one or two things subconsciously which may alter positively the direction of your life.

CHAPTER 2

The Power of Thought

"We are shaped by our thoughts; we become what we think. When the mind is pure, joy follows like a shadow that never leaves."
- Buddha (sage on whose teachings Buddhism was founded)

Our thoughts are already programmed to happen to us and there is nothing we can do about it! True? That's the biggest lie in this universe! If you know any better you will be amazed at the number of people who believe that they have no control over their thoughts, it just happens to them! The best analogy is to get a boat into a river without oars and let the current of the river take you anywhere it wants. I don't think any reasonable human being would do that but in the way we live, that's what we do when we allow our thoughts to happen to us. We create our thoughts and we have lots of them daily, say in the region of between 60,000 to 80,000! We must create our thoughts deliberately and not by default. When our thoughts are by default i.e. we just let them happen, the tendency is for it to stray into the negative territory and the moment that happens it gathers momentum very quickly by attracting similar negative thoughts. It then spirals into uncontrollable monster and you need help to get out of it!

What is the relationship between our thoughts and our emotions? It is a very close relationship because our thoughts create our emotions. In simple terms, thought is the mother of emotion! How? Well, your brain dispenses chemicals known as hormones based on your thoughts and when your thoughts are positive, you get good chemicals to make you feel good. But when they are negative you get the bad chemicals to make you feel bad. Why do we need to know all of this if what we want is just to know how to use our mind to get better results in our business and our lives?

As a growing child, I had spent more time in the hospital than at home according to my parents! I didn't remember any of these at all. I was told that they were very close to losing me at some point. My parents went to great lengths to keep me alive and I am grateful for that and this is part of my desire to do well in the world because I believe, God must have a mission for me to keep me alive. The details I was told were really not pleasant but I am here today and I have lived a life of good health. Despite the fact that I have been relatively healthy since then, I still carry with me the fear of diseases probably due to that early experience of moving me from one hospital to the other!

Childhood experiences may shape our view of the

world, hence the direction of our thoughts. We have to cultivate the discipline to always remain positive. I have got over my fear of diseases because of the knowledge I am sharing with you on these pages. So, if you have any recurring thoughts that you don't want please find a strategy to change it to what you want! It doesn't even matter if you don't know how it came into being; the important thing is to deal with it positively. I usually think that it must have been hard for my parents trying to keep me alive, running from pillar to post. However, I may be aware intellectually but on the emotional level I have no idea of their emotional rollercoaster until the incident that I am about to share with you happened to me and it was the most traumatic one I have ever experienced as a parent and you will see why in a moment!

"Daddy, daddy, daddy!!! I want pasta! I want pasta now!" That is my daughter at the dining table with me demanding that I give her from the pasta that I am eating. She does like to eat with me even if she has already eaten her own food before I am back from work. The day has been so hectic in the office and I am a little tired and just hoping to eat dinner and go to sleep! So she wants pasta and I am eating this pasta with fish sauce and it is really delicious, but that taste is about to turn disgusting in a moment; I scoop a little pasta with a spoon and put it in her mouth! She swallows it and in about 2 minutes she starts crying and in panic I ask her what the matter is and she cries, "*My throat hurts!*"

Apparently, she has a little fish bone stuck in her

throat. So I tried all known methods of getting a stuck object out of a child's throat without success. By now, she is drooling with a lot of saliva coming out of her open mouth. I called the ambulance and off we went to the hospital. I am a bit relieved that at least we are now in the hands of the experts and things should be ok; I feel they would just pick up an instrument and pluck the bone out of her throat! X-Ray confirms the bone is there, but the bad news is that operating on the throat is the only solution. By now I have thoughts coming at me at about 500 per seconds of the consequences of all this. Then I remember that it is not the incident but the interpretation of the incident that determines how well or how bad we manage whatever happens to us. So I go for a little prayer that God may keep this child out of trouble because I can't even live with the guilt if anything bad happens to her as a result of my action albeit unintentional.

When you pray in an emergency situation you feel that God may not answer because you probably haven't spoken to God in a while! So I and God haven't spoken for some time but I still believe if there is anytime I need that once-in-a-lifetime miracle moment, it is right now! The operation cannot be carried out in the same hospital but we have to travel some miles to get to an Ear Nose and Throat (ENT) specialist to do the operation.

The operation was slated for the next day at 4.00pm, so I went back to work to come back by then, whilst the mother slept with her at the hospital. Now I am thinking to myself, what is good about this? How can anything be good as a result of this situation? I feel a certain kind of relief thinking that I would find the positive in this situation whatever the outcome! I don't have any problem when things happen to me directly but it is harder when it happens to those you love but I fill my mind with positive expectation about the operation and believe that she is in the hands of experts and everything will be alright.

Now I know how my parents must have felt when they were taking me from one hospital to the other as a child. I am even more appreciative of their determination to keep me alive in those trying times for them. I went straight to the Throat Clinic from work to be by her side during the operation; I was now in a better frame of mind now than the previous day.

Me: *Good day Doctor, I am the father of Gloria and I want to know if you are ready for the operation.*

Doctor: *You are welcome sir but the operation has been cancelled!*

Puzzled, I ask him why and when is it going to be rescheduled for?

The Doctor says: "*Well, it would no longer be necessary, your daughter is very lucky, the bone has disappeared from her throat and you may now prepare to take her home. She is fine now!*"

That's life! One moment you may be in a state of despair and the next moment is a state of ecstasy at rapid successions as I have experienced in a space of 24 hours! These doctors are specialists and they know their onions and I am sure there is an unseen hand at work in resolving this issue because of my state of mind and believe that things would work out fine in the end. If she doesn't need operation, they wouldn't have referred her to specialists because they are familiar with incidents of this nature. I am sure if they have done the operations it would have been fine as well. It's just the universe way of telling me that my desire for the welfare of my daughter gets the attention of the higher power! I try to learn from my life experience as well as other people's experience with a view to sharing these with my audience so that you are able to avoid making the same and certain other mistakes in your own life if you apply the lessons. Winston Churchill said this and it resonates with me for days and I tag back to realise that it is so true.

"Men occasionally stumble over the truth, but most of them pick themselves up and hurry off as if nothing ever happened." - Winston Churchill

Have you stumble over the truth at some point? What did you do? If you pick yourself up and hurry off as if nothing ever happened, start paying attention to events in your life!

When a life-changing condition happens to you, it may change your life condition depending on how you think and talk to yourself about the situation. I have the advantage that I knew when something bad happens, it is an indication of something good; you may not see it or perceive the positivity immediately. But with time, you will be able to connect the dots! I have experienced certain situation before and looking back later, it is always the right thing to have happened.

So, in future when you encounter a seemingly big challenge, remember that whatever doesn't kill you will make you stronger but only if you cultivate a positive perspective and take positive actions to resolve it or manage it. It is a privilege to be alive and you must not hand your enormous power over to an occurrence in your life because you are capable of conquering anything. Whatever the situation, it is just a little part of your life, so don't let a little part damage the whole by focusing on it in a negative way. Find answers and remember that doctors are not God and their prediction could be way off the mark! How many times in life have we seen doctors' predictions discountenanced by nature and the power of spirit of man? I have personally experienced it first-hand and so many others that defied the prognosis of experts and come out of it smiling. The secret is the power of thoughts and the intelligent use of perspectives.

Life-changing occurrence in life is a gift if only you see it as such. In Bill Clinton's autobiography (***My Life*** – published 2nd June 2005, 2nd edition *Arrow Books*), he says the reason why he is always eager to get things done quickly is because he lost his father very early. He sums it up by saying that if life is that short, the earlier he gets his goals accomplished the better. He became the president of the greatest country in the world in his forties. The way you react to life occurrences is determined by your thoughts about it; some people would say the way you talk to yourself about it. So it is the same, your thoughts are just like talking to yourself; so if you can talk to yourself about issues in the right way then you have the kind of life you want. However, it takes discipline to get in the habit and the moment you get in the habit, things begin to change for good. The secret is the power of thoughts and the intelligent use of perspectives.

Bang! Loud noise then darkness descends and by the time he wakes up, he's in the hospital with jaw broken in three places and mouth wired shut. I played a little bit of football in my time and had a few injuries like swollen ankle and something so less traumatic but the pain was unbearable. That's just me I don't like pains and nobody does! So I thought that was unbearable, but compare this to breaking your jaw in three places; it's unimaginable.

If you rap for a living and your face is smashed it is hard to be positive about that! God says 'I'm about to hand you the world, just know that at any given time I can take it away from you, and so always keep me first.' This is the view of Kanye West about his 2002 accident when he was an up-and-coming producer. Today, he is one of the most celebrated entertainers in the world with tons of money to go with it! The interpretation you give to events in your life will determine your life and such interpretation are derived from your thoughts! Why is the need for these two powerful stories? The power of your thoughts surpasses events, even bad events. Actually, behind every bad event there is a huge turnaround waiting for you to grab it only if you have the right kind of thoughts in response to it. The secret is the power of thoughts and the intelligent use of perspectives.

Do you need a bad event to catapult you to greatness? Not really, but whatever endeavour you embark upon, if it is significant enough, you will encounter challenges; it is the rule of the universe and you must pass the test to rise to greatness. Your thoughts play a great and important role in shaping your attitude and response to life so keep it positive. You can hold only one thought in your mind at a time, so if negative thoughts creep in just change your thoughts to positive and don't go back to the negative thoughts to feel whether it's gone! Just believe that the moment you change your negative thoughts, it's gone for good!

Cultivating the habit of positive thoughts is an exercise that you need discipline to accomplish. In a world of relentless instantaneous barrage of information from all kinds of devices, it is hard to stay positive except you have a system to keep you in check. Listening to news is not good news because no one cares about good news; it's got to be bad to get people's attention. Say between 70 to 80% of news represents stuffs that aren't pleasant and if you are not deliberate in your choice of materials getting into your mind, you are easily carried along the negative trail of thoughts. I still listen to news but the moment it goes on the negative trajectory, I am changing the channel.

Thoughts are energy capable of extraordinary

accomplishments beyond the imagination of man. The power of thoughts has no limit and the earlier you recognise that fact the quicker you are able to direct your life in ways that work for you. Mankind has done extraordinary things in the last 100 years much more than the thousands of years before! Why? We have just started recognising the powers of thoughts and whatever we can think about we can accomplish. I love this quote and it is better to leave it out there without explanation so that you can figure out the deeper meaning you may want to make of it!

According to Augustus Hare, *"Thought is the wind, knowledge the sail, and mankind the vessel"*.

Change Your Thoughts, Change Your Life!

CHAPTER 3

The Learning Machine

"Learning never exhausts the mind"
- Leonardo da Vinci (1452 -1519, Italian polymath who was painter, sculptor, architect, scientist, musician, mathematician, engineer, inventor, anatomist, geologist, astronomer, cartographer, botanist, historian and writer)

Human beings are programmed to learn. From the day a child is born to the day he dies, learning doesn't stop. A new baby is helpless straight out of the womb and from that moment, the learning starts. When he cries, he gets attention and that's probably a good lesson as no one ignores a crying baby. As the child grows, he learns to walk, talk, run, play etc. The challenge for most people is that they cannot distinguish between good learning and bad ones, so the subconscious mind just absorbs everything and this develops into a series of beliefs guiding the individual's life until they decide to change it. What is a belief? A belief is a thought that you keep thinking and it informs your decision on what to do and not do! This has huge implications for how our lives turn out to be; the good news is that you can unlearn the unproductive beliefs very easily if you identify them to be useless to you.

What is the relationship between the conscious mind and the unconscious mind? Your conscious mind is where you put your attention every moment you are awake, it's the part that talks to you all day long, when you are aware of something on the outside, what you see, hear and feel right now and the quick judgment of them are all within your conscious awareness.

Your unconscious mind is where all your memories are stored; it performs all the intricate functions to keep you alive like digestion, regulating your body temperature, healing your wounds, pumps adrenalin when you are in danger to help you make a split second decision to avoid accident and so on. The memories stored by your unconscious start from when you were born and therefore accumulate over time beliefs, patterns and subjective maps of reality that drive our actions or inactions as the case may be.

The purpose of this description is to give you an idea of how powerful your unconscious mind is and how easy it is to use it to get what you want in life by accessing it for transformation of your life. Let me share a personal story of my first-hand experience of the powers of the unconscious mind. A few years ago, there was this meeting of Institute of Chartered Accountants of Nigeria UK District of which I am a member and we usually do this meeting on the last Friday of the month. The meeting is an opportunity to learn and socialise, so I don't miss it. Most times after the meeting we would go to a restaurant with live entertainment to eat, drink and dance, sometimes until very early on Saturday morning! Most of our members come straight from work so they don't drive; a few of us that drive would have to take other members not driving home most times or they take a cab.

On this particular day, the live band was so good that we danced all the way until the morning and I had as much fun as everyone else. So it was time to go home and I had to take some of our members home, especially those living along my route. It was summer time when the sun comes out very early, I think it was around 5.00am in the morning but you could see clearly without the headlights on. So I headed home with two of the members to drop at their respective homes. I dropped both members and they were obviously grateful, wishing me a safe journey home. And you may see why that wish may prove useful.

I usually start my day very early so you may say I am a morning person. I get most of my important work done in the morning. On this day, my day started around 5.00am and here I was, still at the wheel 25 hours after, without sleeping. I am no longer a heavy drinker as I was in my days of youthful exuberance so my head is quite clear, although I have had a drink or two! On my way home there was this tunnel which is extremely narrow and you have to maintain your concentration to stay in your lane without bumping into oncoming vehicles.

At the entrance to the tunnel, I couldn't remember for

how long but I was asleep at the wheel and I only just woke up as I was about to smash into the side of the wall. I still cannot make sense of how it's possible for me to avoid the wall at such a speed. Let me quickly add the fact that I was within the speed limit lest I get a visit from Scotland Yard! I avoided smashing into the wall in less than a split second and luckily, there were no oncoming vehicles so I managed to escape without any dent on my car and more importantly no dent on my sleepy head!

How does the mind swing into action to execute such a miraculous feat without prior warning or prior practice? So imagine what you can achieve if you can call on this part of your mind to come to your aid in whatever goal you set for yourself, that miraculous feat is within your reach and this book will tell you how to do it.

I mentioned briefly in the previous chapter my intention for writing this book. So let me clarify it properly for you. This is actually a business book with a difference, my intention is to teach entrepreneurship in a different way that would not only benefit business owners and aspiring entrepreneurs but also everyday people; you will get ideas here you can apply to your business or to your life as the case may be. I have read a lot of business books and uncountable case studies in the course of my career especially those MBA case studies that may inspire you to create a business of your own. I actually got the idea for my business from a case study but what I set out to do when I started is not what I am doing now but more on that later when we look at how to be in business. My point is not to brag about how much books I have read or case studies I have studied; but it is to make the point that doing business is not the same as reading about it in a case study, so I am approaching this book from the point of view of someone who has actually been in a guerrilla warfare that the business environment could be sometimes. I have an enhanced, first-hand knowledge of the pitfalls and opportunities and I am therefore able to share my experience with you better than a strictly-business-book-writer from abstract and theoretical base.

Let me give you an example you can relate to. I love boxing, I have never laced the gloves but I am fascinated by the idea of the ability to hit someone on the chin without getting hit in return or not getting hit as often! Now there are books on boxing and you can study all the books on boxing in the world but if you have never been in the ring to actually train, you will never be a good boxer, you will not even be a bad boxer either because a bad boxer has actually been in the ring, at least, and may just not be good enough.

The bottom-line is you are not a boxer regardless of how many boxing books you have read. It is the same with business; you are not an entrepreneur regardless of how many business books you have read; you are an entrepreneur because you have started a business. You may not be a great entrepreneur right now but just like the bad boxer, if you dive in and experience it, you will get better and better as you go along and you will find better tools to help you become the great entrepreneur that you want to be. As you read this book, you will realise that it is packed with so many tools and stories that would inspire you to succeed at anything you do whether it is business or not, the lessons you learn here could be applied to other areas of life. Have you heard the saying that 'art imitates life and vice versa' so business theories and practice could also be applied to other areas and I urge you to finish this book and it would change your perspective and outcome for good. So if you are not in business, please know that this book would benefit you just as well.

You may follow all the business books theories and practice and still not get the result you desire, that's the beauty of business; are you wondering how could that be? Well, the reason is the mind-set of the entrepreneur is a very critical factor in the success of the business and therefore my reason for writing this book is to get you in the right kind of mind-set for success rather than slaving away doing more and more and still not getting the result you desire. When things aren't going well, most entrepreneurs do more of what they are already doing but it is unlikely that this would change the situation. This book will teach about what you need to do to get your mind in the right state and then, the application of business theories and practice would explode your results. The way to get the best out of this book is to read it once and then come back to pick the chapter that relates to your current challenge in your business or life. There are also chapters that teach specific skills you may require to accomplish a particular task, so you can jump to this chapter for the approach you may adopt in order to complete such task successfully.

So we say your mind is like a learning machine absorbing everything the senses can perceive as long as it is of interest to you. How do you reach your unconscious mind? Your conscious mind is like the shield for your unconscious mind protecting it from unwanted materials and sometimes from desired outcomes too. To train your unconscious mind to do what you want takes practice and sometimes help. My first encounter with this knowledge is the work of Richard Bandler and John Grinder who studied the work of great hypnotists and therapists like Gregory Bateson, Virginia Satir and others; they document the structure of their skills and make it available to ordinary people. They recognise the powers of hypnosis in helping people with problems like phobias, anxiety, smoking, drug addiction etc. They produce miraculous outcomes as a result helping people overcome lifelong problems in matters of minutes! Richard Bandler goes a step further by helping people overcome their challenges without the need for hypnosis through carefully programmed exercises. I have also studied other geniuses in this field to actually understand how human motivation works in conjunction with the powers of the unconscious mind in accomplishing what we want in life. I delved into the world of spirituality and then manage to align both the science and spirituality to find common ground of actions which may produce result for people. When I talk about spirituality, it isn't about religion! I am a Christian and that's my upbringing but I am open-minded enough to see other people's point of view and beliefs in order to understand it.

The reason why so many people have died in the name of religion is when people think there is only one way and no other way is tolerated! The idea of only one way to reach God has caused mankind a lot of misery since the dawn of time and it would not stop until the end of time. Let's focus on helping people live a better life regardless of the environment where they live. I would not delve into the details of my finding but I would point you in the right direction so that you may go ahead and do your own study and make up your mind, thereby following the path that works for you.

Accessing your unconscious mind is only possible when you quieten your conscious mind and reach out directly to your unconscious mind. It sounds simple but you cannot do it without help! One way to quieten your mind is through meditation because your mind cannot stay in one place for long and it requires discipline to keep it quiet. My first experience of meditation was through the Silva Method and I am still amazed why this program remains relatively unknown; I guess it is because the great people using it may feel that it is controversial and prefer to keep it to themselves. It is actually scientific in the way the program works; I would not go into its details but if you would like to experience it then go and find it on Google. Whatever meditation method you adopt, ensure that you are comfortable with it. When you have achieved the state of calm and quiet; you may then visualise your goals as if you have achieved them. You may need to practise for a while before getting used to the idea but you will get to a point where your visualisation becomes so real, you may not remember where you are when you come out of it. This is my personal experience and yours may be completely different.

Visualisation is important but belief is much more critical if you want to achieve anything in life. When you believe something strongly, every step you take is in the direction that takes you towards the confirmation of such beliefs. Have you seen a perfectly beautiful girl who thinks she is ugly? This is a self-esteem issue and it is a learned behaviour. It would not help her if a lot of people tell her she is beautiful, as long as she doesn't believe it, she would not accept it unconsciously. She may think people are just saying that to make her feel better. So the solution is to change her beliefs about herself talking directly to her unconscious mind. The simple solution to everything else is your ability to talk directly to your unconscious without your conscious mind getting in the way. Everything in life is simple but when we encounter a solution that appears so simple we feel that for it to be effective, it has to be complicated and difficult!

If you think that way even when you find a simple

solution, you will still not use it because we have been wired to think that way, all our lives. My goal is to show people that the best approach to problem solving is to look for the simple and obvious solution when we encounter a challenge or pursuing a goal.

Why do you create shortcuts on your desktop? It saves you time and effort and you are able to reach the program at one click! How about creating a shortcut to solving life challenges or pursuing your desired goals? What are you thinking? You may say it is not easy to get shortcut otherwise everyone would use shortcuts in their life! May be everyone doesn't know they are capable of creating shortcuts to solving their life problems. So if you really want to cultivate the habit of creating shortcuts then start the practice now with small things and your mind will generalise to bigger things and you will find life a lot more fun! Your mind is a learning machine and I want this to sink into your mind such that you will recognise this power and use it to your best advantage. Whatever you train your mind to do, it will do it if you practise it enough and it would become second nature. When I was in secondary school, a quasi-spiritual teacher came to my school to talk about life in general and one thing stuck to my mind and I would share it with you. Have you ever thought you have lost a key and you look everywhere but can't find it; the more you look the more frustrated you become! He advises that you should stop looking for a moment and do other things; then when you come back to look for it; call out the name of what you are looking for, like a key, pen or watch! I thought to myself; don't be ridiculous, that's *hocus pocus*!

So one day I thought I have lost a key and looked everywhere to no avail! Then I remember that lesson and so I stopped looking for it; went away to do other things and I came back into the room and called out "Keys, keys, keys" and bingo I found it within the sofa with the holder sticking out! Surely, that's a coincidence and it wouldn't happen again! Again and again it does and then I use it regularly and I don't care about whether it makes sense or not; what matters is that it works.

So that's an example of shortcut that doesn't seem to make sense but it's a shortcut nonetheless. There is nowhere shortcuts are as necessary as in business and you will see some examples of how some notable successful people applied the principle of shortcut in a simple manner and yet achieve transformational change in results. There is a lesson in the use of shortcuts! You must believe that you will find a shortcut to the solution you are looking for and then start looking for it! Sometimes it may come quick, sometimes you may have to be persistent to find a shortcut or you may elicit the help of other like-minded people to find the solution. When dangerous stunts are shown on TV the usual warning is '*Do not try this at home*!' When I was in school, I was a good student and I try my best to cover my syllabus but when I do revision; I use shortcuts! I figured it out that exams have patterns to it; it has to be because you have examiners who are usually in charge for a few years so they too have habits and patterns; so if you understand their patterns and habits you can predict their questions or at least the area they are likely to test! So I pretend to be the examiner and then pick out questions based on previous questions and the pattern of the examiner! 8 out of 10 times I get it right! My intuition also plays a part in my prediction so that's why I am going to warn you that 'don't try this at school'!

My point is just to buttress the fact that you can always find shortcut in whatever you do in life and it doesn't mean that you should break the law in looking for shortcut because you can always find the appropriate and legal shortcut. Seek and you shall find! Train your mind and play the game of finding shortcuts in little things and soon you will be finding shortcuts in bigger things too!

Life's battle is not won by the strongest or fastest man but one who thinks outside the box; one that does opposite of what a lot of people are doing is likely to rise above mediocrity and have what life has to offer in abundance! Your mind is a learning machine but learn the things that make your life better and delete those that set you back. That is the foundation on which you could build your castle of abundance.

CHAPTER 4

Finding Your Talent

*"In the battle of existence, Talent is the punch;
Tact is the clever footwork"*
Wilson Mizner (May 19, 1876 – April 3, 1933,
American playwright, raconteur, and entrepreneur)

We have talked about your mind being a learning machine and what is called talent is a situation where your mind opens up to absorb a particular skill because you love to do it. The more you do it the better you become; the more people recognise you for that skill the more you are motivated to improve on it! All talents are learned directly or indirectly; no one starts singing the day they come into the world.

There is an advantage in recognising the talent early and growing it but you can learn at any age. Talents like Tiger Woods, the Williams sisters, Andre Agassi, Floyd Mayweather were all prodigious kids in their various sports and they built on the innate tendencies nurtured by their parents! The mind of kids are so malleable and it is very easy for them to learn; when you concentrate all your efforts in learning something exclusively when you are young, then it is completely wired into you.

There is a mental component to all talents, even sports like boxing is more a mental battle as well as it is physical! Don't conclude that sports and music are the only talent-driven avenues that can give you what you want in life; that would be a big mistake! You can find talent in every area of life; if you are very good at doing something so much better than others; something that comes easily to you while others marvel at the skill or hobby, then you have just found your talent.

I am not amazed when I see people make a fortune from just doing mundane stuffs like cooking because I know that it isn't what you do, it is your mind-set! You can make a fortune out of anything and it is all about getting good at what you love to do and find a way to multiply delivering it to a lot of people. How can you make a fortune from just cooking? There are countless chefs and cooks in Europe and US who are millionaires and it's not just by running restaurants but by teaching people what they know through TV programmes, books, Internet and blogging etc.

This is a simple suggestion of how to make a fortune; find your talent, find a way to multiply delivery of that talent to a lot of people in an exciting and entertaining way; regardless of the environment that you live; you are more likely to succeed. Education is great but we have placed too much emphasis on paper qualifications and we teach our children to get good grades, get a job and then they also teach their children the same and the cycle continues. Don't be a hostage to education, get education but know that it is just the basic you need to go out there and learn how to succeed in life. The reason why highly educated people aren't rich is that they are hostage to their education; they have too much to lose if it doesn't work out. In contrast, people who drop out of college have nothing to lose and they just go for it and win. I can write a whole book on this phenomenon because people like Bill Gates, Steve Jobs, Kanye West and other greats dropped out of college and have created a long lasting legacy! People are fixated on working in their area of study even if they aren't necessarily good at it or necessarily love this area of specialisation and they work for 20 to 30 years without fulfilment!

The alternative to this is to find your talent and it is never too late. I am an accountant and a competent one for that matter but I love writing more, I love to teach and I would do both for free. I also love to create things and watch it grow and this is why I got into entrepreneurship so now I am living my passion and I cannot be happier. My knowledge of accounting is so useful in all these areas and I am now having a time of my life! If you find yourself in a profession or trade that's not to your liking, then change it and do what gets your mojo running every minute of the day.

Everyone has a skill they can sell but the challenge for most people is that they have no idea on how to sell it successfully.

What is it that you know how to do very well? (Don't

say there is nothing because if you look deeper you will find it).

What are you good at doing? Some people may falter here thinking it has to be something difficult, academic or technical. It doesn't have to be any of those; it could be simple things like cooking, baking, dancing, physical exercise, yoga etc. I can give you example of people who have made millions of dollars in each of these seemingly basic skills or some may even call it hobbies! Well if you have academic or technical skills as well, it is just as great, so just identify what it is that you are good at doing.

What have you done that other people would respect but also desire to learn and utilise to gain the same benefits for themselves?

What is it that you love to do – this is very important because what you love to do will not seem like work and you will enjoy doing it such that you cannot wait to wake up to do it and you are unable to go to bed with excitement because it feels so good to do them.

How you market these skills is part of what I am going to teach you in this book because if you master this very well, you may well transform your life overnight and the good news is that it is very easy to do because I will give you examples of how to do it.

There is no prescription of how to market your skills, I would just impart ideas that you may adapt to your particular situation; your level of success depends entirely on your commitment towards implementing them.

The quickest way to market your skill is to first and

foremost develop this skill to a level where you know more than other people in this area. This is very important because you want to provide an exceptional service to people, therefore you must hone your skills and really get good at it. I have seen people make millions out of something as simple as juggling. The prerequisite is that you spend time honing your skills to the extent that you are really conditioned to improve constantly. If you see top performers like Beyoncé, Rihanna, Chris Brown etc.; they spend hours rehearsing and when they come on stage, we marvel at what they are capable of doing! Humans can learn anything and get good at it and it is even easier if it is something you love to do.

The foundation is to be good because if you are promoting mediocrity there is no chance that you will get to the top. Look around you to survey your immediate environment for someone who is really very good at that skill and has managed to be very successful; if you have more than one, that even gives you option to pick on the appropriate model that suits you. If anyone is successful at anything there is a structure to what they do whether or not they are aware of it. If you look hard enough you will know what the structure is! Adapt the structure to fit your unique situation. I have studied some individuals who have successfully mastered the art of marketing their own skills and have acquired a fortune in the process. The common denominator is that they are all seen as an authority in their field.

It isn't that difficult to become an authority as you may think but it requires a plan. In this day of social media, there are rules you may follow to get you in the heart and mind of people! The easiest way to do this is to teach what you already know. You may think that what you know is not enough but if you follow the previous advice about honing your skills; you must by now be a kind of miniature expert in this area; whatever you know is good enough because there are so many people who don't know half as much. Have you heard about what is called 'the curse of knowledge'? The moment you learn something you assume that you have always known it and interestingly you may also think that everyone else knows it too! So don't suffer the curse of knowledge as what you already know may be important to a lot of people who are completely unaware of it. I have said this before and it is worth saying it again that your skills may not necessarily be academic, but if it is, there is nothing wrong with that. The important thing is that you get good at it.

When you teach others, you are saying to them that you care about them and more importantly you are also saying that you are very good at what you do. You are likely to build a following if you provide value to people free of charge. These people would become your advocate when you get to the stage where you need to market your skills. I would give you an example of someone who has used this to amass a fortune! Jamie Oliver is a chef and he owns a chain of restaurants but the bulk of his wealth came from teaching people how to cook on TV and he has now added activism to his repertoire and politicians of diverse ideologies are queuing for his attention. He now promotes healthy eating among school children. You must look beyond his cooking skills; he is a consummate self-promoter and his bank account is testimony to his astuteness in marketing.

Martha Steward accumulated hundreds of millions teaching home making tips on TV and her fortune is mainly from teaching people her skills; her core competence is in teaching in an entertaining manner not just the home making skills; so cultivate your communication skills to become an authority in any field!

The two examples are from TV broadcasting but now we have a leveller; the Internet has given the underdog an opportunity to excel which wasn't available some thirty years ago; so we are living in a time of unlimited opportunities and you must grab yours by taking actions. Start your authority journey today and see your situation change sooner rather than later.

Create a product
This is not necessarily a physical item but a product could be a service, a book, an app, a lesson etc. Make sure the product is what people want! How would you know that? Ask yourself! What would you like to buy? Simon Cowell says the secret of his success in music is that he produces music he loves and assumes that if he loves it other people are likely to love and buy it too. He applies the

same rule to his TV programs; 400 million dollars and still counting for him, that's a good rule in my book!

Market your product online

This is the easiest and cheapest form of marketing to get your product out there to a lot of people. The Internet is getting a bit crowded these days and to get your products out there requires a skill and there are unlimited resources out there on how to do this successfully. The challenge with prescribing what works right now is that you may be reading this book 10 years after it is published so my advice is that you must spend time to learn what works as at the time you are reading this book. Start implementing what you can find and don't look for the magic bullet because there is none; but keep an open mind about learning new things every day and you will succeed. I have engaged in online business for a long time and I know the rules change constantly so make sure you are up to date in what you do. If what you are doing is no longer working then investigate and change it and continually search for new methods that get results.

Befriend the media

The best way to get something from someone is not by begging for it or appearing needy; that never works! Have something to offer the other party! The media are no different from other companies, they too have a need, the need to find news, information, sell adverts, beat competitors etc. How can you help them to achieve any of these goals, no matter how small? You may just find out that they are willing to help you too. I write articles for newspapers, I do radio programmes teaching entrepreneurship and I grant interviews to TV stations. All of these didn't happen by accident! So find your ways of getting in the public eyes even if you do it for free initially, the reward would be immense thereafter due to the growth of your personal brand. Richard Branson is so adept at using the media that he spends less on advert probably than most other brands but still get his companies on the lips of everyone. Some people think that David Beckham is not eloquent or very smart; they are so wrong! If David Beckham writes a book on how to use the media to your advantage today, I would pre-order more than a hundred copies and give to all my business partners! Why? No sports star or celebrity get more column inches in the UK than Beckham and his wife! Anyone who thinks all of this happens by accident is very naive indeed.

On the back of these skills to manipulate the media, his wife Victoria is now a *bona fide* designer in her own right, she even designed a car! This is getting a bit out of hand if Victoria Beckham is designing a car! But if you have seen the **Range Rover En Voque**, it was claimed to have been co-designed by Victoria Beckham! That's a ridiculous brand stretching! My point to you is that if you want to be the authority in your area you need help and no bigger help than the media. Find a way to make yourself relevant to the media and you will reap the reward bountifully.

Launch Your Product
This doesn't need to cost a fortune, which is very important! Online launch is the cheapest way to do this and there are so many strategies for doing this. You may research the most suitable one for you. It isn't a quick fix, you need a website to launch your product so get one as soon as you start creating your product. Get your potential customers' email addresses and it is not as difficult to do as you might think. The best way to gather your list is to offer your visitors something irresistible free of charge in exchange for their emails and you may grow this very quickly. Don't buy list because it would just be some random emails which may not be your target audience.

When you have gathered your list, don't bombard them with sales emails daily. Provide useful information to your audience free of charge, be tactical in using this to generate response from your audience and build a bond with them. Sell them what they want by asking them questions about the product and you will be surprised that people do engage when you make them feel important.

When you launch a product, make sure you set a time limit like three or seven days after which they cannot get the product any longer. This forces people to make prompt decision otherwise they may just procrastinate forever.

Offer your customers some incentives to refer their friends and family to buy your product

Provide after sales service to ensure that your customers are getting the value you intended; you will be surprised that your customers are very keen to provide you with the much needed feedback you want.

Marketing your talent is not as difficult as you think and if you follow the ideas here and do your own research, this may just be the beginning of your own transformation. When you operate in your area of talent and you do the best you can, then you will become unbeatable.

CHAPTER 5

Generating ideas for a new business

"Creative thinking inspires ideas. Ideas inspire change"
- Barbara Januszkiewicz (1955 - , American painter, artist's filmmaker and creative activist)

Thou shall not steal. So states the Bible. Rubbish! I am talking about ideas for new businesses, if you wait until you generate a brand new idea no one has done before you will probably wait for ever! Of course, some geniuses have done exactly that and they changed the world as a result but the reality is that you only ever have people like Thomas Edison, Henry Ford and Steve Job etc. once in a generation. So, for us mere mortals we can steal ideas from other people and do it better than everybody else and build a successful business as a result.

Ideas for business are everywhere. If I drive one kilometre in the inner city of London, I would find more than 100 different businesses on both sides of the road;

everything you see represents one business or the other but the point is for you to find that single thing you are passionate about! Having advised that you should steal business ideas, it may seem a paradox to you that I would also advise that you don't follow the crowd. Well, bring something new to whatever industry you are getting into to distinguish your products or services.

Let me share with you some examples to shatter the notion that new ideas are so complex and difficult to come by and you must be a genius to come up with one! The way our brain works is that once we focus on something we start to see more of it. I love cars but I don't care how it works, the gadgets, the engine and so on; what informs my decision of choice of a car is the external beauty. Period.

By the time you are reading this book, you may ask: what is he thinking because more beautiful cars would have been made. The first time I set my eyes on the BMW X6; I said to myself I must get one! Well, that's it; everywhere I go there it is! I began to notice the car everywhere. This system is called Reticular Activation System (RAS). This system helps keep us sane because it filters out those things that aren't important to you and you only see what is of interest to you. The moment you decide in your mind that you are seeking ideas for new businesses then you start to notice what you hitherto wouldn't have noticed. One good idea is what you need and the moment you have decided, things would start to fall in place for you. Really? Yes, that's what I have personally experienced in my own business. I have done many businesses in my life; I always think of doing business as a kid and I have had many adventures along the line. I usually have a business on the side either run by me or by someone else, so I like the buzz, the uncertainty, the joy of creating something and helping people! I knew instinctively that doing business online is an attractive proposition because of the potential reach of the Internet and the cost effectiveness of the process. This idea is in my head until one day that I read the quote below.

"The moment one definitely commits oneself, then Providence moves too. All sorts of things occur to help one that would never otherwise have occurred. A whole stream of events issues from the decision which no man could have dreamed would have come his way. Whatever you can do, or dream you can do, begin it. Boldness has genius, power, and magic in it. Begin it now." Goethe

I started writing my business plan immediately after reading this from a book and I carved it out, frame it and hung it in my bedroom. Today I am proud to provide employment for a lot of people and this book is an extension of the dream to make a little difference in someone's life no matter how small. I hope it does the same for you. That idea in your head, is it writing a book, starting a business, volunteering, starting a course or whatever it is that's been at the back of your mind, now is the time to bring it to life.

Going back to generating ideas for new businesses; a simple idea may create a brand new industry. Hip-hop is now a phenomenal success with worldwide acceptance as a music genre! DJ Kool Herc is credited as creator of the rap element of hip-hop by experimenting with *deejaying* as he named the art at the time. Imagine how much influence, wealth, employment, power and so on that emanated from this single idea. It is a fascinating story and if you want to know more about it you may go on *YouTube* or any of these channels as I don't want to distract you with long story. What is in your head that you think is so stupid and people would criticise you if you dare say it let alone do it? Go ahead and do it because you may be creating a new industry as a result.

In my country Nigeria, when growing up I see women sell iced water, yes iced water! They carry a bucket on their heads and measure a cup for you and there are a lot of customers for this business because of the heat and humidity. Well, it is cumbersome; it is sometimes unhygienic but the fact remains that people are buying it. We stay back at school to play football in those days and the women selling iced water are like God's gift to us. After hours of running around kicking and chasing the ball, we would queue and wait patiently for our turn to get the cup of iced water. The fact that the water may not be completely safe never occurred to us. This 'iced water in a cup' business went on for as long as I can remember but about 18 years ago, one man thought to himself that since there is a demand for this product called iced water, why not pack it in a cellophane bag and make it easier to distribute and charge a little more than iced water in a cup that has been around for decades! He called it 'pure water' and the demand was astronomical and still going on!

I am a bit curious about the name 'pure water' but that's what it is still called today and the business keeps growing with competitors intensely active in the market. Meanwhile, given that some of the brands are so less than pure, regulatory measures had to be put in place by the authorities who must give you a licence and a (registration) number to be able to produce them these days!

How long the forerunner of this venture enjoyed the exclusivity of his idea is not important because weeks after it came out about 100 companies, small to medium, started churning out 'pure water'. This tells you that to generate a new idea is not about sophistication or ingenuity but simply by observing your environment and looking for ideas you may improve, tweak or edit to make it better. That's my first-hand experience of how easy it is to generate new ideas but let me give you two other examples you can easily relate to. Does the name Jeff Bezos ring a bell? Probably not, except if you are an Internet entrepreneur. Well, what about him you may ask?

Jeff Bezos observed the rate of growth of people using the Internet at the inception of the technology around 1994 and thought that it would be easy and cheaper to sell books exclusively through this medium. Bang! He created a monster! Have you heard about

Amazon.com? Well even those people living in the Amazon have heard about this company created by a man who followed his dream. In his own words, there was no certainty that the idea would work and it was even more risky for him because he left a very lucrative job in Wall Street to jump into the unknown world of new business in a new industry! Today he has written his name in gold and he would be an inspiration for generations to come.

Perrie Omidyar also thought of putting the age old auction on the Internet platform in 1995 and similar to Jeff he also created one of the biggest companies in the world. Have you heard of *eBay*? This is another giant of a company that has grown bigger than some reputable companies that have been around for centuries.

How complicated is it to sell books online and how complicated is it to put auction on the Internet? These ideas aren't out of this world and anyone could have thought of them but these guys didn't only think of it they went ahead to take the risk and they did it! You can generate your own ideas too and when you have found it don't wait, just go ahead and do it! Do it now!

The way to be successful in business is to be in business. What does that mean? I would illustrate with a story of Richard Branson who started business by publishing a student magazine and then started selling records. Following this with broadcasting, he set up a radio station, only to establish an airline and several other businesses. Most of them are successful but not all of them are successful, but that's not the issue. What this tells you is that the moment you start a business, whatever it is, you will find better ideas and better tools as you go along. Richard has a philosophy about business that is very appealing to me; he thinks business should find a way to help people have fun and it should also be fun to actually do the business! I also follow this philosophy in my own business.

I would tell you about my experience to clarify this idea for you in a way to get you started whether or not you think you have the perfect idea or not. I got the idea for my new business when I was studying for the MBA and we had a case study on eBay which opened my eyes to the enormous opportunity of operating business on the Internet. Having read that case study, I thought I would create an auction platform in an emerging economy which is Nigeria and I started writing the plan for it. When I researched into the Nigeria market, I realised that effective online payment was not in place yet; but now, I cannot stop so I created a classified platform for people to upload their products and sell to customers free of charge. It was very popular but we weren't making any money and advertisers aren't in tune enough with online marketing to patronise us on such a scale to sustain the business. We then started **MannaStores**, a procurement and logistics company helping Nigerians buy things from UK/US and delivering to them anywhere in Nigeria. That's our breakthrough and now we are really in business creating opportunities for others and providing employment for young people which was my original goal of going into business. Since then I have been involved in training both technical and soft skills, I have a radio program teaching young people to get excited about business and how to succeed using all the tried and tested methods that worked really well for our company and other lessons that we have learned along the line.

Now, let's go back to finding the right ideas for your business. You will never have all the answers until you have braved the odds and start. If you don't know this, Richard was branded as dyslexic by his teachers (i.e. people who find it difficult to read and spell) yet today he is a billionaire. So, don't let your limitation stop you from starting a venture that would be useful to the community and provide the right kind of challenge for you.

There will never be the right time, the right circumstances or the right people to help you. That is certain but if you start right where you are, you will find a better tool as you go along. In this book, we would share with you some of the challenges you are likely to face as you start and how to overcome them. I don't have all the answers for sure, but I will guide you to a place where you will find the answers relevant to your situation

Going back to our idea of observing your environment for ideas, if you look around you, it is likely that you will find simple ideas that would get your ideas juice flowing. My goal in sharing this message with you is not to tell you particularly how to start, though I would give you the tips on how to start. What I want to achieve ultimately is to inspire you to start, the moment you start you cannot stop yourself even if you try to do so. I am now going to tell you simple steps you may follow in order to start a business.

1. Write down all your ideas of business on a piece of paper

2. Rank your ideas based on two criteria - What do you love to do? What is it that you are good at doing? If you are able to align both questions then you have found your passion

3. Pick one of these ideas and start writing a plan of how to start

4. Find someone who has done similar business successfully and copy what they have done (without infringing on existing copyright and patent rules). In this instance copying is allowed! When we were in school, during tests and the examinations period, some people were very good at coping other people's answers! We called people like that names such as 'giraffe' or 'Rank Xerox' (after the copying machine giants) or copycats! This act (of dishonesty) was frowned upon by the school authorities and rightly so! In real life, you are allowed to copy business ideas or strategy that has worked well for someone else.

Actually, if you approach successful business owners and ask for help, they would be glad to share their ideas with you; this is exactly what I am doing with you through this book. So don't be afraid to copy. Alternatively, buy a book by the entrepreneurs in your area of business.

5. Start the business with whatever tools are available to you and you will find better tools along the line.

6. You must build momentum and sustain it. What does this mean? When you have started you must do something daily towards the commencement of this business no matter how small. What this does for you is build momentum to the extent that by the seventh day you will be so energised that when you encounter temporary setbacks, you will be able to bounce back immediately

7. Vision: You must see your ultimate goal in your mind's eye in order to internalise it. This is not new and it is called visualisation and it helps your brain align with what you are capable of achieving. The reason why visualisation works is that (in my own experience) when you want to do something new, your brain will send you a warning sign that this is not familiar. So in feeling the fear, you either steer clear of that new thing or it prepares you to confront it with energy. When you visualise, you are making

those goals familiar to your brain so that when you think of the goal you will not get the warning signal. This enables you to take the step you need to achieve the goal. By the way, this is my own analysis and you don't have to accept or believe it but one thing I want you to believe is that visualisation works and it has worked for me times without number.

8. Motivation: To be good at anything you need the motivation to actually do the thing that you need to do. When I started my business, I knew very well that I needed motivation to keep going, so I bought some audio books which would help every stage of my growth in this endeavour. For instance, there are audio books teaching how to start a business, how to grow a business, autobiography of entrepreneurs, how to manage crisis, how to market your product or service online or offline etc. Today as I speak to you if you have Internet connection you could get all these resources free on *YouTube* or via *Google* search if you prefer reading materials. I prefer the audiobook because it allows me to listen and learn when I am doing lesser tasks that don't require much concentration.

I have told you many things you must do to ensure that your business takes off easily and safely. I am usually fascinated by how aeroplane takes off with hundreds of people and tons of cargo, time after time without fail. It is down to science and there are things that must be in place for this to happen without any incidence. Equally, there are rules about flying i.e. things that must not be done and if you do them it's either the plane would not fly or it would crash. For example, if you overload a plane beyond the capacity weight that it is stipulated to carry, it may crash. Business is no different, there are things you must do to succeed especially at the beginning and there are things you must not do!

1. *Don't kill your idea by telling a lot of people about it before it is entrenched in your psyche.* When I wanted to start my business, the first person I told about doing business in Nigeria baulked at the idea and told me how it is going to be hard, how risky it is and his bad experience of doing business in our country. Ironically, this friend of mine is a motivational speaker. I respect the fact that his advice was not intended to discourage me but rather he is concerned as a good friend for me not to make a bad business decision. Well, it was too late for me to back out so I didn't listen to him; instead it reinforces my determination to succeed. I am lucky that this is my natural response to suggestions from anyone who says 'oh you can't do it' for whatever their reason may be; I would only dig in more and put in more effort at doing exactly that.

2. *Don't quit your day job abruptly without money to sustain you for a while as the stress from not being able to pay your bill will kill your motivation and put you in a state of despair.* The theory of motivation by Abraham Maslow and others talk of hierarchy of needs, which means if you are unable to achieve the lower level physiological needs of eating, clothing and shelter, it is extra hard to achieve the higher psychological needs of self-actualisation which is the need you are trying to satisfy by starting a business. I don't want this book to be academic in any way, shape or form; the only reason why I refer to academic theories is if they enhance the readers' understanding of my point and by the way, I would have simplified it into a language everyone would be able to grasp easily.

3. *Don't bet your house on a single idea!* What?! Yes, I am not saying you shouldn't take a risk or even take a big risk but just don't bet your entire life on it succeeding. Things do happen in this world that's completely outside our control so have a Plan B. Just in case! The alternative is to ask others to join you and if you convey your ideas very well, you will get a lot of offers. I would look at how to raise money in a subsequent chapter in a way that you have probably never envisaged that money could be raised.

4. *This is slightly related to the previous point (Number 3). When you invite people into your business, don't give too much*

of your business away because of desperation. Value your ideas and what you are bringing to the table. I will cover this on the subject matter of raising money for a business whether existing or new.

5. *Don't employ family members you cannot sack if they don't perform.* Please don't take this advice if it doesn't align with your culture as it is based on my personal experience and observation. My half-sister is very close to me and she lost her husband when her two kids were four and three years old. The husband went to work on that fateful day and didn't return by 6.00pm which was the usual time he comes back from work. My half-sister, worried at this out-of-character scenario, went to the police to report. But on her way back, she saw a large crowd gathered at a man shot dead which turned out to be her husband! The killers were never found. This man couldn't hurt a fly and was probably at the wrong place at the wrong time. This was some two decades ago and I have always wanted to help my sister raise the kids. I told you the story so that you may understand my motivation for trying to groom her kids for the future. One of her daughters left school with a National Diploma and I thought it would be a good idea to help her get experience in an office setting and then grow from there. To cut a long story short, she wasn't cut out for an office job as she comes whenever she wants, very slow to learn, very difficult

to control and was just a complete nightmare for the manager. The manager wanted to sack her but being my niece, he was reluctant to follow this path. The last straw that broke the camel's back was a physical fight with the manager; so I did let her go with the consequent family rift that came out of it. So perhaps, this is an isolated case but now that's my rule, I would rather support the individual financially outside my business than bring family members into my business. It is even more challenging for a new business because you need no distraction at this stage of the business.

6. *Don't be fearful of the future.* Trust me, whatever you do, you are going to get some things wrong if you are in business and that truly is the least of your worries because the price of doing nothing is greater. So when you have made the decision to do something in business or even in life, go for it with every fibre of your soul to get the right outcome. Henry Ford said that the most important of his three principles of success is this:

"An absence of fear of the future or of veneration for the past. One who fears the future, who fears failure, limits his activities. Failure is only the opportunity more intelligently to begin again. There is no disgrace in honest failure; there is disgrace in fearing to fail. What is past is useful only as it suggests ways and means for progress."

The last paragraph should prepare you for what is coming next which is the biggest stumbling block for people with good ideas but it doesn't have to be and after reading the next chapter, you must be energised enough to start putting the suggestions into use immediately.

CHAPTER 6

How to raise money for your business

"When I was young I thought that money was the most important thing in life; now that I am old I know that it is"
- Oscar Wilde (1854 –1900, Irish author, playwright and poet)

One of the biggest excuses people have for not starting a business is the lack of capital or in simple terms, lack of money. In this chapter, I want to share with you some simple ideas on how to overcome the issue of lack of money, or insufficiency of it for your start-up. Have you heard the term *'its only money that makes money'*? Well, that's not true. Money is useless if you don't have a plan and the brain to implement the plan. There are also companies that are in the business of supporting people like you with ideas but no money and my advice is that you should check in whatever country you may be reading this book what is available in your environment.

I have observed that those who have created some of the biggest businesses in the world today were not born into great riches and at the point of starting their businesses needed the help of others to make the dream a reality. What they have got though was more powerful than money; it is called initiative and persistence - that special ability to walk through brick walls to get what you want. Some people are good starters and they put a lot of energy into their work and then the inevitable happens: a challenge, an adversity or an accident stops them in their track. Reaction? Quit! Then they start something else instead of gritting their teeth and continue on the path that may well lead to the achievement of their goals. The new endeavour they have started would also run into the inevitable brick wall and then they quit again only to start something that would be a bit easier, and so the pattern continues. They then look back at some stage and feel they have been unlucky or dig up other excuses in extenuation of their successive failures.

Failure is not the problem. Most people don't even give themselves the chance to fail because each time there is a challenge, rather than confront it, they withdraw. Those who have done great things never quit no matter what the challenges may be! This is about raising money for your business so why the whole talk about initiative and persistence? This is to prepare you for what you may encounter in your effort to find the funds to invest in your business; so when the inevitable challenge arises you will be aware that quitting is not an option.

The story is told of how a young student in the United States started a business in the University and fifteen years later, he had become a billionaire. There are slight variations in the success narrative of this entrepreneur, but the context is true enough to teach you the lessons intended. I am not saying you will achieve the same level of success so quickly but whatever your goal is, it is important to show initiative and start taking action on your idea.

The name of this student is Mark Cuban. At the age of 12, he sold sets of garbage bags to save up for a pair of shoes he liked. In high school he earned extra dollars any way he could, mainly by becoming a stamp and coin salesman. You can tell from these activities that this young man knows in his mind that whatever he wants he is capable of getting it by just doing something about it. Most people are waiting for the big break to happen to them instead of going out there to make it happen. So the story does not end here,

When Mark was in the university, he had a dream to start a nightclub and he needed $15,000 dollars to do so. He started calling banks from his dormitory to borrow the money. Of course, no bank would lend a student that sort of money to run a nightclub. Mark knew that too but he won't let that stop him. By a stroke of luck, an uncle overheard him passionately describing how the club would be the best in town and all that, so the man said to him: "Mark, if you don't get the money from the bank please come to me." Of course he didn't get the money from the bank but the uncle provided the money and the club was so successful that he became well known. However, this was not how he made his big money, with a taste of that success he dabbled into internet ventures at the inception of the technology and built the first website to show sports and other entertainments online. He named the company *Broadcast.com*. Yahoo would later buy the company from him for $5.7billion!

These events took place in a little over a decade from the inception of the nightclub to becoming a billionaire! If you conclude in your mind that he is just lucky, you should stop reading this book because it means you are not in a state of mind to understand the message that I am trying to convey to you. Of course, you aren't going to stop because you know there is more to this story than just a question of luck. Mark himself said he is the luckiest man alive and he is not wrong in saying so, but he made his own luck through initiative and persistence. I am going to enumerate the lessons so obvious from the story and by the way, you should extract your own lessons from your own perspective. Dare I say the lessons are useless if you don't use it? I am not saying you should use it at some future date when it is convenient for you or when the time is right or when the opportunity arises. No, use it now and that's how to get the most out of this book.

The lesson I want you to learn from this story is to be implemented immediately:

Mark from the early age believes that whatever he wants he's capable of getting it - from the example of selling rubbish bags to buy a trainer as a kid. You can develop such belief too and it doesn't require you to be a genius to do so.

Mark takes action on his ideas even if the action seems fruitless to an onlooker, he knows that those actions themselves may not produce the desired result but the actual process may lead to resolution of the challenge – the example of calling the bank to borrow the $15,000 dollars that he knew to be a long shot. However, the initiative to call the banks produce the money albeit indirectly because if he doesn't call the bank the uncle is unlikely to know what he's trying to do and the dream would have ended right there and then before he has the opportunity to test it.

Go after the big stake – there is no way *Broadcast.com* could have made him a billionaire but he is astute enough to know that Yahoo's perception of the probable competition may cause them to offer big money for it and he's right! Yahoo never got the commensurate return on the bold investment but that's business; they are still here today doing a lot of great things in the industry.

Mark acts on his instincts without any delay – you can do the same. Mark is not a genius, he has no special talent. He's just another bloke like you, the only difference is that he has developed plain gristle and bone; this rude, simple primitive power called persistence; if there is any secret to his achievement; there it is! Read that again and again and again; internalise it and you too could do what he has done in whatever endeavour you find yourself.

I will highlight five tips on how to raise initial money for your business and like Mark, some or all of them may not give you immediate results but if you are single-minded and continue pursuing them with persistence, something will show up for you

Write a business plan – if you need a structure of how to write one please search on google.
Evaluate from your business plan how much money you intend to raise

Make a list of 10 probable sources of raising the money- don't judge the probability of whether it is possible or not just try and take actions on the ten sources and be persistent in your follow up

Use Other People's money -From your list of 10 above, there must be people you know who would trust you enough if your idea is good to invest in. Ensure that you repay if it is a loan but if it is equity ensure that you reward them for their faith in you

There are some companies or government agencies set up to fund businesses like yours so search for them and follow their rules.

The next path on this journey is those tricks and tips to ensure your success in raising money when you have to pitch your idea to potential investors. Money in itself is useless if it is idle so nobody wants their money to remain idle. Therefore, this is your number one belief to assure you that the potential investors are not necessarily doing you a favour. It is a symbiotic relationship where both of you derive benefits from the transaction. If you have done a good job with your business plan, the uniqueness and profitability of your business and the industry should be emphasised. I am going to reveal to you a secret that has been used to raise hundreds of millions of dollars without stress; but my advice is that you should test it and make sure you are good at it before approaching potential investors. The secret applies to other areas of life as well if you want to apply it as a tool for influencing people. People don't make decisions based on logic most of the time, although we think strongly that we do! Emotions play a great deal of role in our decision making process. The way our brain processes information would also determine what we pay attention to and whether our decision is swayed one way or the other. The information you are about to read is powerful, I must emphasise that you use it for positive goals and when you have raised the money; ensure that the stakeholders are fairly rewarded for their faith in you. I always like to arrange my thoughts structurally such that it is easy for my reader to implement or remember.

These are some of the ideas to give you the approach for communicating your ideas to a potential investors and practical things you should do to get results.

Authority – The concept of authority is to help us comply with the societal values therefore we are taught to respect and follow instructions sometimes without question from authority figure. At home you do what your parents ask you to do most times. At school you follow the instructions of the teacher and at work you follow the instruction of your manager and you may add your own examples; this is universal whichever culture you look at. Let me add the fact that authority in some cultures is much more hallowed and less so in others. What you need to get out of this is that when you are seen as an authority in any field, you can easily influence others. Let me give you a practical example of how this plays out in real life. In Nigeria there is traffic light at some intersections but there are also traffic warders directing traffic at some intersections. The traffic warder is probably on minimum wage in some cases so outside his job he has little or no authority. Now let's assume a millionaire is driving his Rolls Royce and the traffic warder waves him to stop at the intersection.

At that point in time the traffic warder has the authority and the millionaire who could employ hundreds like him has to obey. So what has that analogy got to do with raising money? I want you to know that authority is not necessarily static, you could influence the situation by usurping the authority just for the moment that you need to and then hand it back after you have got what you wanted. There are many ways to usurp authority and you are creative enough to find what is convenient for you; but I would tell you some examples of how I have used this in the past. I was working for a company years ago and a bigger company was in the process of taking over our company. I was the Director of Finance and Corporate Resources at the time and I was vehemently against the takeover. Please don't ask me why I was opposed to it but I have my reason which cannot be published. The CEO of the bigger company arranges a meeting to see me about the finances of our company and to discuss my objections. Please note that we are the smaller company and the CEO of the bigger company has all the powers and authority in this transaction. He arrives at our office like 10 minutes early and I have seen him from the window of my office so I closed the door into my office before he walks into the main office where the Administration staff work. My P.A. knocks to tell me the CEO is here to see me; well the normal thing to do is to ask him to come in straight considering his authority as the potential CEO of the Group. If I ask him to come into my office straight even though he is some minutes early I would have handed the authority to him so I politely ask the Office Assistant to tell him to wait and I would call him when I am ready. So I have flipped the authority status on its head at that point because ordinarily he shouldn't have to wait. He is probably not used to being asked to wait, so from the subconscious level I have scored the first point in the influence game! Another point is that when he walked in I didn't apologise for keeping him waiting because doing that will hand the authority back to him. So I just welcomed him and I could see that he was slightly nervous, so Round 1 belongs to me. When you have usurped authority at the beginning and so early in the encounter, you are more likely to get what you want from that transaction.

For obvious reasons, I am unable to disclose the details of our conversation and the results but I got the outcome that I wanted from that meeting just by that small act of defiance. Now, you have to judge the situation you find yourself in and decide quickly what small action you could take especially at the beginning of the transaction to flip the authority status in your favour and that would set the tone for the rest of the transaction. You may use this approach not just for raising money for your business but for other kinds of transactions which involve the need for you to influence others.

Get in the right emotional state - If there is anything you must learn in this world, it is your ability to get in the right emotional state when you have to! Performers are acutely aware of this phenomenon and the very good ones get it right all the time; the average ones less so! I was watching a TV program sometimes ago following the artiste Nicki Minaj on TV. Yes, it is a bit of a guilty pleasure but in doing so, I wanted to see if there is anything that grabs my attention which may help other people. Swear words and raunchy displays as you may well be aware are not unusual when Nicki Minaj is about! She keeps emphasising the fact she must rehearse at the venue where her next concert is supposed to take place. But the problem is that the venue is not ready (for use) and may not be ready until the night of the concert. The manager suggests that they could arrange the rehearsal in another location but Nicki was having none of that: she insisted on rehearsing at the venue. I thought to myself that what is the fuss about rehearsing at the venue? As this thought was going on in my mind, she said: "*If I don't rehearse at the venue, then I may be nervous at the concert and that's not gonna happen because I cannot afford to let my fans down.*" Eventually, the event's organisers caved in and she rehearsed at the venue in its uncompleted state and at the show, she brought the house down!

Just a small confession. I am a big fan of Nicki Minaj and whatever you think of her, she works very hard coupled with the fact that she has phenomenal talent. So, what can you learn from it? Accomplished performers have a way of getting themselves in the right emotional state before their performance and it doesn't matter how they achieve that but each individual devises their own way. I would say to you that you must devise your own way of getting in the right state that is unique to you. Some people just get in the right state by their nature but majority of the people are not like that, so find your own unique method.

That said, there are some tried and tested methods you may adopt to give you instantaneous result. When you are doing anything new for the first time, please rehearse, rehearse and rehearse! Why is this necessary? The purpose of the rehearsal is to familiarise your brain with the new situation so that your brain doesn't send you the wrong chemicals that would destabilise your emotional state. Let me tell you how this works so that you will take it seriously! When you encounter a danger or think you may come to harm or a feeling of being judged, you feel anxiety! The emotion of anxiety grows bigger if you stay in that state and this would prevent you from concentrating on the important thing you are doing at this particular point in time. Your thoughts generate your emotions and your emotions also generate your thoughts! It starts with your thoughts, so please whenever you feel anxiety you are telling yourself the wrong kind of stuff, just change it. Have you heard that we can only hold one thought in our head at a time and that the moment you change your thoughts from negative to positive you start to feel better?

You may also have a mantra and the one I use most often is this *'If God be for me who can be against me'*. The interesting thing is that it may sound simple but it is very powerful but then that is if you believe it.

Use Rituals – Athletes are very competitive and that's just stating the obvious. It is important we learn simple things from other areas of life and apply it to our business. This can only help us get better. Athletes train for many years just for a 10 seconds race. Wow! Imagine the pressure to perform that they face in lining up against each other knowing that everyone on the line has worked so hard for, say four years, in the case of Olympic and they are after the same thing you want! If the emotional state you are in for any important occasion is critical, this is the place and situation to test it. The athletes that are top performers that I have observed have rituals. It may be explicit such that competitors can see it or implicit such that others may not see it!

Rituals may be physical or mental and I think using both physical and mental rituals work better but it depends on individuals. Let me give you some specific examples of top performers who use this method, not just before the games but during the game when the stakes are very high like taking a penalty in a big football game or starting a 100meters race or taking a free kick etc. Watch the American track and field sprinter Tyson Gay start a race; he goes through some physical rituals which is the same all the time. Even when there is a false start, he goes through the ritual just exactly the same way for the re-start. Watch Ronaldo take a free kick, he measures the distance between him and the ball and it is the same number of steps every time, he stands akimbo, he takes a deep breath and look at the corner of the post, run to the ball for the kick and most often than not he scores. Usain Bolt jokes around at the introduction of

100m race and when it's time to start, he points at the heavens, does a sign of the cross and he is ready. I am only telling you about their explicit rituals but what about their mental rituals that we don't even know about.

Let's move away from Athletes and look at some outstanding performers like the iconic British television presenter and entertainer, Sir Bruce Forsyth who was on the top of his game even beyond his 80th year and with decades of successes! Please go back and watch his entrance before starting any show, he walks in and does a double skip and he says when that happens its 'show-time'! So what is going to be your 'show-time' rituals that when you do it you are in the zone?

Why am I telling you all this? If you are not in a good emotional state, you cannot convince anyone to invest in your business because body language speaks louder than voice. The reason why I am emphasising this is that the biggest hindrance for most businesses is the inability to raise the money to actually start therefore if you get this right, then you have conquered one of the stumbling blocks preventing most people from taking actions on their ideas! By the way, this method could be used in other areas of life where you have to be in a confident state.

Mental rituals – Our bodies are intricately connected to our brains and the reason why athletes have physical routine is linked closely to re-creating the emotional state they have experienced before and the purpose of those physical movements is to bring that specific emotional state at this point of the competition. This pattern is similar to the intuitive act of crying by babies when they want attention, they realised very quickly that crying gets the attention of the mother (and the fathers sometimes!). I am a father of three lovely kids and I am a very hands-on father but when my baby is crying the mother has an instantaneous pacify in the form of breastfeeding, so primarily babies cry for their mother more often than not! So our brain detects any linkage we associate with any particular event and we sometimes allow this to happen by default instead of deliberately creating the association we want between an emotional state that we want and the physical act of our choice. Let me give you a practical example of how this works, I am not afraid of anything except one 'Mr Snake' and every time I see one I freeze and go into a state of panic! I know intellectually that it is not all snakes that are poisonous and they would not necessarily bite you if you don't upset or confront them, but instinctively I react with fear. I have no idea why this is the case because other people don't feel the fear exactly the same way I do, so it is my brain and the interpretation of a perceived threat at that particular point in time.

My brain is so programmed to keep me alive because if I don't particularly know which one is dangerous or not then I am better off to feel the fear and flee! Now, I consider this as a positive device to keep us alive. The problem with this phenomenon is that we sometimes generalise this fear and extend it to other areas of our life where we don't need to feel the fear because there is particularly no threat to our life! So how do we sort out when an event is a threat to us or not? This would be a complicated thing to do and I believe the best approach is to just find a way to feel the emotion we want to feel when we need to be in that particular emotional state. Seriously, the world has lost a lot great talents to stage fright or 'camera fright'! It is important that we programme our children to be able to feel the emotion they want when they want it.

I am a football fan and I support Arsenal FC. Let me tell you a story of how top performers do mental rituals to be in a good state to perform when they need to! Jens Lehman was our goalkeeper at some point and he was a top performer but he left for Germany as age was catching up with him. He was there for sometimes and then one January transfer window Arsenal's manager, Arsene Wenger brought him back to the club as a cover goalkeeper. He was on the bench for one of the matches and in the middle of this particular game, the number one goalkeeper had an injury and couldn't continue. So Jens who at that time hasn't played competitive games for months must now come in as the substitute goalkeeper. He performed excellently well, conceding no goal and the team won! At the end of the match the TV crew approached him for an interview for his excellent performance, asking him the secret of such performance having been out of the game for a while! I was expecting him to say: '*Oh I have been working so hard since I came back bla bla…*' but no, Jens said when the manager asked him to warm up to substitute the injured goalkeeper he went through his last match in Germany in details as he was warming up (this was to recollect his great performance). This is called visualisation and it gives him the confidence to put in such a great performance. The lesson here is that you can re-create any emotion you have felt before by reliving those experience and you will feel the emotion when you want to. Confidence is a most powerful emotion that would help you get whatever you want in life.

You don't need to be confident when you are brushing your teeth in the morning or taking your breakfast because it is not needed for the task you are doing. When you want to go out there and tell someone to invest in you, then you need to feel confident about yourself first and foremost and then you need to feel confident about your idea so that you will be able to convey it in a convincing manner. How did it feel like the last time you were super confident and you feel you could move the world? Access that memory and relive it in vivid details. Remember how you breathed, how you sounded, how you stood or sat and how you looked. Make the picture clear in your mind and if you concentrate on this for a moment you will notice that you start to feel confident, now link this feeling to any physical act like clenching your right fist. Be in this state for a little while and then distract yourself. After a while clench your right fist and see if you now have the feeling of confidence. If you do this properly you should be able to bring back the confident feeling.

Now for some people it may happen very quickly but some people may have to practise this for a while and for the benefit you may derive, please do the exercise several times if you have to. When clenching your fist brings that confident feeling then you have done it. When preparing for your meeting with investors, clench your fist to get the confident feeling then rehearse your pitch in that state of mind. Visualise your meeting with potential investor and imagine everything going perfectly well. Do this several times and you should be able to accomplish delivering your pitch when in a good state. Does this mean you will get an investment instantaneously? Maybe or maybe not, but what you have done is that you have given yourself the best chance to succeed by preparing very well.

I love gadgets and I jump on the bandwagon of new smartphones every time a new one comes out. They are wonderful little things with a lot of functionalities. My enthusiasm ends with buying them and the first three days are very important because if I don't familiarise with the functionalities within that time frame, that's it: I am not going to use all the arrays of apps that can do wonderful things. Our brains could be compared to these wonderful smartphones, the apps and functionalities are there for your use whether or not you use them. Our brains are so powerful with so many functionalities and 'apps' that we never used in a lifetime!

It has been said that we rarely use 10% of our brain capacity! We have done wonderful things already just using 10% of our brains, what would happen when we find the clue to using more percentage of this wonderful organ? The fact that you don't use the apps and functionalities in your smart phone doesn't mean they are no longer working. So, anytime you are motivated enough to explore them, they would work as intended without any question. Our brains also work the same way, the fact that we haven't used them for a long time doesn't mean they won't work whenever you switch that part of your brain on for any purpose. So our brains are powerful beyond measure and so are we; this knowledge is enough to give us the confidence that we are capable of achieving anything we want.

Trust – If you are trying to raise money from an individual, you must earn the trust of this person to have a remote chance of influencing them to part with their money. You may earn someone's trust indirectly if another person they trust introduces you. At the first meeting, you must also present yourself in a credible manner through your appearance and communication. I have spent a lot of time on how you could prepare mentally to project an air of confidence and credibility. If you appear to a stranger hoping to invest in your business and you are visibly nervous then you have lost the chance. A little bit of nerves is acceptable as it prepares you for what you intend to do but the moment the nerves take over your brain it's difficult to come back from it. The quickest way to lose credibility is to be so nervous that you lose your senses and it is not unusual as even some top politicians have suffered what is described as *brain freeze* at press conferences and trust the media to have a field day at the expense of the politicians. Familiarity breeds trust and if it is possible to get to know someone a little bit before pitching business to them it would help tremendously. Another way to lose trust quickly is to make outlandish claim of the potential of your business. When you do projection, make sure you show that the business is worth investing in, but don't go overboard with unrealistic profitability projection. What should be the structure of your pitch when presenting to an investor? There are key dos and don'ts that I would share with you:

Time frame – Human beings' optimum attention span is about 20 minutes without a break so if you go beyond this time frame for your pitch, it could be counterproductive because you need to keep the attention of the investor on you and the moment concentration wanes, you are in trouble because the likelihood of influencing them diminishes with every additional minutes beyond the 20 minute mark. Let me share with you some examples of my observations with this particular concept. My favourite entrepreneur is Steve Job in terms of attention to details and visionary qualities. When the first iPhone was launched, for the first time in the history of technology, three key products were combined into one i.e. an iPod, a phone and internet device. Well, I am not here to talk about iPhone sophistication or the technology; I just want to show you why your pitch must not be more than 20 minutes. The presentation by Steve Job himself introducing this ground-breaking product took less than 20 minutes, if you are in doubt, go on YouTube to check and it was the best presentation I have ever seen. The language is simple and the demonstration is clear. There is suspense, surprises and without any shadow of doubt, there is magic, such that the crowd went crazy! That's the genius of Steve Job.

I am telling you this so that you don't make a big mistake with your pitch thinking that the longer it is the more chance of influencing your potential investors. Create a structure that is unique to you but my advice is that you start with introducing yourself, your big idea, explain your figures and unique selling proposition and then make your offer. Practise this several times to ensure you can do it effectively within 20 minutes.

Warning- Don't approach the investors in a needy state of mind! I learned this lesson early in life that pity doesn't get you anything significant... In my country Nigeria we have a lot of beggars on the street and you cannot miss them. They make a living somehow from the generosity of other people. I am not condemning the beggars or making judgement as to how they got into the position. At times, a few tend to demean themselves to attract attention or engender pity from the passers-by so that they could get a little bit more money. Most people are usually turned off and instead of getting more money; they get less! It's like a hard sell and when it appears like emotional blackmail, then it doesn't work. So what this has got to do with raising money for your business is a warning that you shouldn't go to the investors in a needy state of mind. Don't make it seem like your life depends on it. People will only invest in you if there is a benefit for them not because they have pity on you especially if a lot of money is involved. So be prepared, be confident and be yourself.

Follow up – most people are good at starting an endeavour but then after going after it for a while with limited success then they give it up and start something else. If you are serious about raising money for your business you will get a knock back several times and with the belief that every *No* that you get moves you closer to getting a *Yes*, there is nothing you cannot accomplish. When you get a *No*, don't blame yourself - just know that what needs improving is your process. Just go back to the drawing board and have a go again. Raising the money is not the end of the challenge, it is just the beginning. No amount of money you raise will be enough, so you must be able to plan and forecast your activities. Get an accountant to help you with this part as it would help you make the right decision with the money at your disposal.

CHAPTER 7

Business Environment

*(**How to succeed in business regardless of what is going on in your business environment**)*
"No one can possibly achieve any real and lasting success or 'get rich' in business by being a conformist"
- J Paul Getty (1892 – 1976, American industrialist and founder, Getty Oil Company)

When you ask a business owner whose business has failed to say the reason, in our experience as consultants, we get bundles of reasons associated with the environment. It could be down to government policies, the economic downturn, rapid changes in technology or change in consumer behaviour etc. These reasons may be valid and true; however, the only reason businesses fail is solely down to the owner of the business. The earlier you recognise that fact the quicker you are able to take responsibility for your business and a quick turnaround is just around the corner. All the reasons given for business failure would continue to affect businesses but if you recognise and plan ahead of time, then surely you will be able to envisage the impact of these factors and take actions to manage them effectively.

What is the most important factor in business? As it was hundreds of years ago, so it is today; getting customers at little or no cost. It is not as difficult as most of you think and it has nothing to do with the type of product you have or the kind of business you are in! Let me give you an everyday example, fast food restaurants are common place in this country and almost everywhere in the world. This is a business that people can go into with little capital so therefore the competition is stiff and it has been so for a long time. Thousands of restaurants have been started in the last 50 years, but why is it that Macdonald's has been so dominant? The secret is actually not a secret at all; it is down to the skills and strategy of the entrepreneur. Why are you reading this book? You want to learn a new skill? You are already in the top 20% of business owners likely to succeed.

Let me warn you that learning the skill is only half the battle; the other half is the discipline to actually implement it. Some people read books, attend seminars, courses and webinars; they listen and agree with all the facts but they never implement what they have learned. Have you ever been in that position before? Probably! I would not only show you what to do but how to implement it easily.

Analysing your business environment is an exercise to help you make the best decision to succeed in your business and the measure of your success is based on how your customers react to your offer! The quote above talks about not being a conformist if you want to 'get rich' or simply put, succeed in your business. Being a conformist means you are following the crowd; the problem with that is that it is crowded where the crowds are and your opportunity is limited! I am not talking about which sector of business you want to invest in or your industry! I am talking about your strategy as an entrepreneur; think different - be different.

Travelling in London during summer using the underground is not the most pleasant experience; sometimes the train is so crowded that you can stand in this fast moving train without holding on to anything because other bodies are supporting you; sometimes you cannot even scratch your face because passengers are packed in like fish in a sardine tin! The train operators' attempt to address this problem is to devise what they call peak times and off-peak times. During the peak hours, you pay more for your ticket for travelling than you pay for off-peak travel times! So, this attempt doesn't work as you might expect because of the human nature to follow the crowd. We like to conform sometimes subconsciously to what everyone around us is doing and there is a time when this is useful but not when in business. I prefer to avoid the crowded train so I wake up early and I have two or three seats empty either side of me and I wonder why people don't take the option of the off peak early travel rather than be packed like herded sheep during peak times.

It is the same when I drive to work! When you travel

early, the road is free of traffic and the only thing stopping you is the traffic light and it takes me 20 minutes to drive to work instead of 90 minutes during peak times! You may ask why more people don't take the option to travel early and enjoy all the advantages of convenience and more importantly time-saving afforded by not following the crowd? Majority of people love the morning sleep but if you don't follow the majority, the road of opportunities is open to you and you travel free of congestion, and people wonder why you are so successful in some endeavours where other people struggle.

The metaphor of the road of life is no different from the road we travel every day. As you travel the road of life, you must keep your ears and eyes open; look around you constantly to spot opportunities and avoid threats, use your knowledge of the road and learn new routes; always find a quicker way to reach your destination by acting smart without breaking the speed limit; keep your focus on the road, make adjustments, stay in lane, change course when necessary, slow down, speed up, follow direction, try new routes, travel off peak times, give others a chance, take care of the car and more importantly enjoy the ride of life!

Now let's talk about the business environment and how to understand it such that we could make the most of the knowledge to transform our business and indeed our lives. Having analysed the environment, you then need to design a non-conformist strategy to exploit the opportunities and avoid the threat as a way to navigate forces intelligently that are seemingly out of our control successfully.

In the last 20 years, the business environment has changed dramatically and I would show you the movement in a moment. *Yellow Pages*, *Loot*, catalogues, flyers, newspapers, radio and the television etc. are some of the media that once wielded enormous influence on commerce. The influence of these media is rapidly diminishing and the new era of Internet media is gradually taking over the business environment. The Internet media is not the easiest of field to navigate and it is a crowded arena but the opportunities are huge if you know your way around it. Getting your message across is more difficult because the levels of distractions people are facing are enormous. How do you stand out from the crowd? How do you spend less and get more for your money? How do you measure what you are doing? How do you use the technology to skyrocket your sales? How do you consolidate your success? We would teach you all of these and more as we go along.

As I have explained above, it is a new media and the rules have changed. When I say the rules have changed, I am not referring to 10 years ago or five years ago or even one year ago. It is changing so rapidly that what worked for you a few months ago may not work today and that's the sort of challenge facing business owners but how do you wade through this web (pun intended) of confusion to get the best outcome for your business? For example,

Facebook changes the way you see information constantly to ensure people remain on their platform. *Google* does the same, they know the powers they possess and they are making the most of it for themselves. When you understand the rules, you must also understand how to exploit the rules for turning your prospects into customers.

Let me share with you one secret known to great minds that you may adopt today to change your business. Analysis of data gives you the roadmap to success and this has created one of the biggest companies in the world. When *Google* started, the two young founders were PhD students, so they knew this fact and used it! When people searched at the time, they get varied results without consistency. They analysed the data and found that the websites with the most links from other websites are usually the most relevant and popular; so they design their search criteria to rank search results to reflect it! The result was astonishing as this catapulted them into the Number One search engine and they have never looked back! The rest, as they say, is history!

How does this apply to me as a small business you may ask? That is the next template I want to share with you. It is called the SWOT Analysis! When you analyse your business, you will find out a lot of things which give you the direction to go and what to do immediately to get good results. So review the template and answer the questions. Use the answers to design your plan; implement your plan and see your business grow!

BACKGROUND

SWOT' is a commonly used tool to take stock of where a business is and how it could improve. But it can also be used by individuals to recognize our unique skills, strengths and talents. Use this exercise to help you manage your weaknesses and threats while taking advantage of strengths and potential opportunities - and grow your business too!

NOTE: This exercise is not about being modest or overly self-critical. For maximum impact, answer the questions honestly – and remember to think about it from both your perspective and those around you.

Planning is one of the exercises business owners think

STRENGTHS	WEAKNESSES
What do you do well? *What do you do better than others?* *What unique skills and talents do you have?* *What do others see as your strengths?* *What are you proud of, like about yourself, enjoy doing?*	*What could you do better?* *What do you avoid?* *Where do you have less skill or talent than others?* *What are others likely to see as weaknesses?* *What do you need to face up to?*
OPPORTUNITIES	THREATS
What opportunities are out there for you? *What trends could you take advantage of?* *Which strengths could you turn into opportunities?* *What is going on locally that you could capitalize on?*	*What trends and threats could harm you?* *What is your competition doing?* *What threats do your weaknesses expose you to?* *What obstacles do you have coming up?*

is a waste of time. They jump into the business and just grind away. If that is you, take a deep breath and sit down to plan. Now it is not a 50-page plan; your plan could be on one to three pages! Are you thinking how that is possible? Well I have been teaching summarised business plan to business owners with unbelievable results. So I would teach you how to do a one page business plan. I recognise the fact that you cannot actually get customers without a plan, therefore your business plan would tell you what to do to get the customers you want.

What should you include in your business plan?
Your Vision -Start with a dream of where you want your company to be in five years' time; dare to dream big and inspire your team by sharing this dream with them. Imagine the success your company would have achieved in five years and document it as you want it to be.

Promotion- Plan your promotional activities and find creative, less expensive options to promote your business. It is unlikely that traditional methods of promotion like TV, radio, newspaper etc. would be suitable for a start-up or small to medium size company. Find creative ways to reach a lot of customers and the Internet is a useful tool but you must learn the rules and measure your outcome constantly.

People - First rate people hire first rate employees and second rate people hire third rate employees. I have said this before and I would say it again that finding the best people is the most important task of an entrepreneur and this would give you great mileage if you do it well. Do have a plan on how to do this well and if you need help of professionals go for it! Any amount spent on finding the right people is an investment for the future of your company.

***Finance*-** Cash is king as they say so you must plan your money and evaluate what is going in and out to be sure that you don't run out of cash abruptly as that may be difficult for a business to cope with. If you can afford it, an accountant would do a good job for you in this area. There are a few templates you may adopt if you do a search for it online to help you do a Cash Flow Projection, Profit and Loss Account etc.

Systems and Procedures - You must have systems and procedures which you may create with your staff to address recurring tasks so that your outcome may be standardized for quality purposes as well as protecting the assets and resources of your company. You must plan this ahead and carry your team along. Let me show you how standardization may help your business prosper. The MacDonald's beef burger that you eat in London is exactly the same as the one you eat in US or China; the cheese burger you ate last year is the same as the one you ate yesterday! Do you imagine this is by accident? You can only achieve such consistency through strict systems and procedures implementation. This consistency and clever marketing strategy is what put MacDonald's ahead of competition; though others are now copying their strategy but they have already established dominance. Please refer to the topic on *'Systems and Procedures'* for more information.

Competitors - Analyse what your competitors are doing and there are a lot of resources online to help you do this effectively. Don't be bogged down by what competitors are doing just use their activities as a guide for your actions so that you are not left behind. Make sure your focus is how you can do better than they are doing in specific areas where you have competitive advantage.

Combine your answers to the questions in the SWOT Analysis and break down your plan as above and write your business plan. Don't make it a huge story just basic actions that you intend to take towards each of your objectives in each area. In doing so, you may end up with 2 to 3 pages which would focus your mind and help your implementation.

Your plan is useless if you do not implement your action plan so after your plan you must focus on implementation. You must also periodically review your progress and make changes where necessary.

CHAPTER 8

Branding

When some business owners hear about branding they think of logo, name, adverts, strapline etc. This is not the way to think of your brand! Let me illustrate with a beautiful building that is well designed and with good ambience all round. The substance of the house is not just the paint, the paint just enhances it. So the superficial things like logo, name, strapline etc. are like the paint, but the real substance of your brand is the quality of your product or service. If you have a good product then the superficial stuffs would enhance the brand name; but if you have a bad product it would only remind them of how much they dislike your brand. If the structure of your building is weak, it doesn't matter how beautiful the paint or exterior ornamentation may look, when it crumbles the paint doesn't matter. So, the way to build a great brand is to build a great product or service.

Branding, like any other thing you do in business, requires serious planning and you must decide your positioning in the market. What is your focus in terms of how your business is perceived? The scenario below illustrates a typical example of a unique brand.

Customer (thinking aloud): *How can this shoe I bought 6 months ago break right in the middle; I have really used this shoe though but if someone has to replace their shoes every six month; that's too much of a budget for shoes especially if the shoe is really very expensive. I am going to call this company that sold me the shoe and complain, this sounds like a rip off to me.*

So John picked the phone to call the company that sold him the shoes!

Customer Service: *Good morning, my name is Charles. You are through to Zappos.com, how can I help? May I know your name please?*

Customer. *My name is John. I bought this expensive running shoe six months ago, now it is broken right in the middle and I cannot use it anymore, I am really upset about this considering the cost of the shoe.*

Customer Service: *Hey John, I am really sorry you have any reason to complain about the shoes we have sold to you but where is the shoe now?*

Customer. *Well, it is here with me but it is completely useless I cannot return it so what is the point?*

Customer Service: *We do take responsibility for the products we sell here; could you please give me your customer number and the invoice number for me to trace the product? I would stay online for you to find it! I would send you a brand new replacement and with a token gift that you have any reason to complain about our product. We source from top manufacturers but things do go wrong sometimes and we would give feedback to our suppliers.*

Customer. *How do I return the damaged shoe?*

Customer Service: *You don't have to return it; you may* donate it to the homeless if you want. The replacement shoe will be delivered to you first thing tomorrow morning. Is there anything else I can help you with?

Customer: *Wow! Nothing, I am really surprised and happy with your service. Thanks for sorting it out!*

Customer Service: *It is a pleasure, we are always here to help 24 hours of the day and 365 days of the year for our customers, so if you need anything, give us a call. It doesn't have to be me any other staff will treat you with the same level of care. Do have a wonderful day John!*

Let us analyse this scenario –

The customer is unhappy about the product

The customer already used the product for six months

Then, he called Customer Service

Compare this transaction with other companies that you know as of today and tell me any of them that treat customers as good as this.

Other Companies: Return policy -14 days or no return at all on some products

Zappos' Return Policy – 365 days to return. Their CEO said jokingly that they are keen to serve everyone including the procrastinators so you can take your time in deciding whether you want to return or not!

Other Companies: Phones answered by machines and your time is wasted choosing this and that option and eventually you wait for another 10 or 15 minutes; sometimes you just don't bother to call them anymore!

Zappos: One call straight to someone who resolves your problem

Other Companies: You can only return items in their original pack otherwise it would not be accepted. It doesn't matter whether you like it or not! You can be as unhappy as hell; we have got your money!

Zappos: Items returned are accepted with apologies regardless of the state of the item and new one sent to customers. It's not written in any rules but staff are allowed to use their initiatives! The only rule is that the customers are happy!

Other Companies: The attitude of some customer service staff can be so frustrating that they argue every inch with you about terms and conditions and why you didn't read 10 pages of small print before buying a £10 item! I have faced this scenario time after time! If I have to read every terms and conditions before buying anything online, well I would not have time to do anything else in my life!

Zappos: Pleasant and courteous Customer Service Staff with the attitude of total care for the customer. No silly terms and conditions in the treatment of their customers.

Other Companies: There is a culture of making as much money from customers as possible right now!

Zappos: There is a culture of long term view of supporting the customer with the view of keeping the customer for life! This works better both in the short term and the long term than ripping customers off at the slightest opportunity because they can actually do so legally.

Let's review the impact of this type of branding through good customer service. Zappos.com started by selling shoes and they decided right from the outset that they aren't going to spend a lot of money on advert but they would let their customer service do their adverts for them! This company got to one billion-dollar sales mark in about their fifth year without spending a fortune on advertisement. Now that's what I call branding, because their customers are so loyal that they tell their friends and family about this great company that is so caring they don't mind making a loss on a transaction as long as their customers are happy! The truth of the matter is that you cannot make a loss when your customers are happy. This story below further illustrates how Zappos distinguish themselves from other companies.

In January of 2000, a customer emailed to describe her recent Zappos shopping experience. She tried ordering two different pairs of shoes, both of which were unavailable, but that wasn't why she made the contact. It was the fast, courteous response of the Zappos Customer Loyalty Team as well as receiving both a gift certificate and a t-shirt for the inconvenience that wowed her. That feedback changed things for Zappos: What if the company focused not solely on what it sold, but how it sold it? What if Zappos focused on wowing its customers? "We asked ourselves what we wanted this company to stand for," said CEO Tony Hsieh, "we didn't want to sell just shoes. I wasn't even into shoes - but I was passionate about customer service." So you want to build a great brand, build a great product and a great customer service to go with it. I will give you a template for building the structure to create a great brand.

FOUR QUADRANT BRAND MANAGEMENT

How do you position your Brand in the minds of customers - Brand Messaging?	*How do you deliver on your promise to the customers?*
How do you align your product and service with the needs of customers?	*How do you build a culture of great customer service?*

When you have designed your business around the four quadrants here then you now get the paint out to decorate your brand. Now you get yourself a good logo, strapline, great name etc.

Brand Message - What do you want your company to be known for? In the example above this company is known for great customer service. So make a decision on the perception you want to create in the minds of your customers.

Delivery – This is very critical. It is where you plan your operations to ensure your customers get what they want all the time and when you falter, forget about profit and make it up to the customer.

How do you align your product and service with the needs of customers?

Ask questions from them and use the answer to provide and design your product or service. Study the trend in your industry because the needs of your customers are always changing! Implement your solutions to your findings

How do you build a culture of great customer service?

If you operate as a sole owner without staff then this is easy, but when you have to employ people then you must find people with natural tendencies for empathy and are good communicators!

Document your findings and implement immediately and you will be surprised at the result you get long term. If you are thinking, what about now, I want results now. Yes, you will get result now if you act immediately, so my first statement is just a tease to get you to understand that immediate action is required for both short-term and long-term results.

CHAPTER 9

Procrastination: The Killer of Dreams

"Procrastination is like a credit card:
it's a lot of fun until you get the bill"
- Christopher Parker (1983 - , English actor and television presenter)

Human beings learn all kinds of stuff growing up and this is what makes us human and the learning doesn't stop because we are old; it is a lifelong privilege. Yes, privilege! The habit of procrastination is a killer of dreams and the danger of this habit is that it creeps on you without knowing it. When you intended to do something important and you find a very plausible reason not do it right there and then; you are hooked! The interesting thing about this habit is that it is learned. Some people are so good at it that it becomes second nature and if that is the case, it takes a lot of mental strength to shake it off.

Now, it is also easy to shake it off, but you must first recognise that it is present in your make-up (and this is difficult to accept). Be true to yourself because admitting that it is something you learned to do and that which you can also unlearn, is your first step towards stopping it! No one is born to be adept at procrastination, it is a learned habit. It was said that Henry Ford's final interview with his candidates for senior position involves having a dinner with them. The table would be set nicely and the food served with array of condiments and salt. Now he observes that those candidates who add salt to their food before tasting it are likely to implement plans without testing them. No matter how good this candidate had been up that moment, he would not employ him. The lesson that I have picked from this is that the way people do small things is the way they would do big things.

Well, we are talking about procrastination here, so you may just as well wonder what the relevance is of my correlation between little acts and taking major decisions. Well, procrastination is not limited to big things, when something turns into a habit; it permeates all spheres of your life. In a quest to set things right, the first step could be an observation of how quickly you do small things; this may indicate whether the habit of procrastination has crept up on you. When someone makes a habit of this, it then goes to affect how you deal with major decision which may affect your life. I will come back to this concept later, but let me share with you a true life story and you can then make up your mind whether the price to pay for procrastination is really worth it because taking action is easier than procrastination. James (not his real name) was my friend in the adolescent years. He was a brilliant young man but also the happy-go-lucky type. You will like him instantly as most people often do. James' family are relatively wealthy. The father was a contractor but he had many wives and lots of dependants. In the traditional Nigerian culture, if you are wealthy, it is an unwritten rule that you take care of other extended family members. Besides, such relatives may also stake a claim on your estate in the event of death. This practice varies from one culture to the other, so it is not generic. In my community, it is not unusual for extended family members to share the property of the deceased regardless of the number of children left behind. James sat by my side in the classroom and we were really close so I knew how brilliant he was. At that time in Nigeria, you spend five years in the secondary school and then sit the school leaving certificate examinations. We took the WAEC (name of the exam and conducting body then) in the same year but when the results came out, they were generally bad for most people. However, James' results were exceptional but for English Language!

He wanted to be a doctor and he already told me he made a bad mistake immediately after writing the paper - that he forgot completely to attempt one whole question worth 25 marks, and he didn't realise it until after the exam. He felt that he had let himself down badly but he got A's in most of the other subjects including the dreaded Physics, Chemistry and Maths etc. James father did what a father would do in such situation; congratulated him and asked him to re-sit the English language next year. James spent most of his time in my house and the parents were very much aware of this and sometimes I spent time with him too. So, James' father gave him money to pay for the exam and he did promptly and he kept the teller. He needed to go back to the school and confirm that he had paid because his name was already in the list for a resit. James stayed in our house for most of this period and on odd days when I would ask him if he had confirmed his payment, he would say to me: *'Well, I still have time. I would go tomorrow or next tomorrow or even the day after.'* This went on until the submission closed.

Ordinarily, he had paid and his name was on the list, so in an ideal world he should have been registered for the exam. Fate has a way of playing intriguing tricks on people in life and sometimes we must double check especially if this is something that is very important. If James had double checked, whatever the mistake was would have been corrected before the closing date. So he was well unaware that his name on the list had somehow disappeared for reason no one knows! James was gifted and didn't necessarily work as hard as everybody else but still excelled. I have never seen James work as hard since we have been friends for years, he worked his socks off preparing for the exam. During this time, James' father fell ill so he had to juggle caring for the father with studying because he was the father's favourite kid and as his health deteriorated, James couldn't leave his bedside but he nonetheless kept his preparation going. Unfortunately, not long after, his father passed away! James was devastated because he was so close to his father. James was quite ambitious and despite his father's death he mourned for a while and went back to preparing for his exam. He desperately wanted to be a doctor and English Language was his only obstacle.

So closer to the exam date, he had to go and pick up the identity card at the school. However, he was about to get the shock of his life as they searched for his name on the list but it wasn't there! Disbelief, anger, despair and sadness all rolled into one huge emotional roller-coaster for James. He would later tell me that he contemplated jumping into the deep trench near the school and that could have killed him. The story of the trench is interesting and I cannot resist telling it. Before colonialism, there was a lot of inter-tribal wars between towns and cities, so as part of the strategies to protect the town they dug this massive trench around the town. Then, the soldiers will hide strategically around the pit to attack enemies coming to invade the city thus preventing the invaders from capturing their men as slaves. It must have been a fearful way to live in those days. So my school was built very close to one of the trenches and we marvel at how it was possible for men to do that with simple implements to protect their town and their people. So James lost the opportunity to retake his exam. This was the time in Nigeria when the moment you gain admission into the university, you become the responsibility of government in terms of feeding, books, accommodation etc. This was the good old days of our country.

What happened afterwards was more challenging than it seemed initially. James' extended family took over the property of his father and they shared it among themselves; leaving the children in poverty. James went to the College of Education to study Physics and he eventually got his degree and he is now a professor but I spoke to him recently and he still feels he is not fulfilled because he lost the opportunity to pursue his first love which is to be a doctor. So just two hours of non-initiative caused a lifetime of unfulfilled ambition.

Back to my submission of how people do small things is the way they do big things, I have tested this and realise that it is true for me. The habit of prompt action could be developed by starting with small things like you look at your shirt in the wardrobe and you think it needs ironing, why don't you just pick it up and iron it. Let's say you finish eating instead of dumping the plate in the sink, you just wash it straight away. Your desk is messy and you don't like it; some people like working that way so if you are that inclined by all means do nothing but for those of us who don't like working in a messy environment, just clear your table and arrange it. When you do this, you are cultivating the habit of doing things promptly and you will get used to the idea of personal initiative. Having read this you will agree with me that it is true and logical;

you may even start doing those things immediately but it takes time for habit to form, if you do it for a few days and abandon it you will quickly revert to your old ways. This quote gives you an idea of how habits are formed and I love it:

"Habit is a cable; we weave a thread of it every day and, at last we cannot break it"
- Horace Mann

It takes around twenty-one days to form a new habit; the idea will become entrenched and you will then find it difficult to revert back to the old procrastinating way. When you intend to do something quickly and an excuse pops into your mind, kill it immediately, especially when you are trying to cultivate the habit of doing things quickly. I read a book on dealing with procrastination and the simple submission is that the moment you encounter a task you know you must do just say 'do it now' and it warns that when you say it you must do it. It is very simple enough and it would have a good effect in developing your personal initiative. Make a list of what you need to do at the beginning of the day and review at the end of the day whether you have done them or not. If you haven't done them for good reasons don't beat yourself up on it, just ensure that you move those items to your next day list and do them first; that way you are clearing the potential blocks which may frustrate your attempt to develop personal initiative.

Personal initiative and prompt action is the way to move gradually towards your goals and nothing will happen overnight; because climbing a rock is not something you can rush and that's the way it should be. It is a natural law of nature, move gradually towards your goal and enjoy the process rather than the outcome. Why do you think that some of those people who get a windfall from lottery or sudden fame encounter turmoil in their lives? The reason is that it overrides the natural law of nature and therefore it requires more effort and wisdom to deal with sudden rise than gradual rise. Some people even lose the sudden money quickly because their brain cannot adjust to the upheavals accompanying such windfall.

So start now by doing the smaller stuffs on time and it would spread to other areas of your life; you would have developed a new habit that could propel you towards your goal whatever it is.

As the age-long saying goes: *"A stitch in time saves nine"*

CHAPTER 10

The Lessons of Momentum

"If you have the guts to keep making mistakes, your wisdom and intelligence leap forward with huge momentum"
- Holly Near (1949 - , American singer-songwriter, actor, teacher, and activist

The way things work in this universe is so orderly and when you look at nature you can learn a lot from the simple observation of events. What I would like to show you with the lesson of momentum is that, small action builds your momentum gradually; the continual application of this action generates greater action to build towards your ultimate goal. When we wake up early in the morning and look outside the window you can hardly see the light but gradually the light increases until light turns into heat and it gets hotter and brighter throughout the day. In Africa, rainfall also starts gradually with a light shower and then it increases until it becomes a heavy rain! Let's observe how a car builds momentum from starting speed to top speed: it is a gradual yet continuous application of force.

How can you adopt this analogy to help you in your decision making? Any goal that you want to achieve begins by taking small action, no matter how small and then schedule subsequent actions to follow until you have built enough momentum so that you are unable to stop even if you want to. In my business, I have an example of a young lady who extricated herself from unemployment to becoming an employer herself. If you have been nursing ideas for several weeks, months, years or even decades but have done nothing about it, then this should inspire you to do something about it. When I started my procurement and logistics business **Mannastores Online**, helping Nigerians buy goods from UK and US, and delivering to their doorsteps in Nigeria; a young woman came into our office in Lagos because she saw some of our adverts in the paper that we help businesses buy things from UK and deliver to anywhere in Nigeria. She is a graduate with a degree in Chemical Engineering and very bright indeed and I got very close to her as her little initiative impresses me a great deal. I tried my best to support her but she was so self-motivated that she really doesn't need any encouragement. In Nigeria graduates are required to undergo national service for one year after tertiary education in a scheme called the *National Youth Service Corps* (NYSC). This lady had completed the programme two years before she came into contact with us and she had been looking for jobs without success. Most Nigerian (fresh) graduates are in similar position but she wouldn't wallow in self-pity; so she came to our office to meet the Business Development Manager and asked for advice on what she could do with the little money she has in her savings account - at that time about N100, 000 (Naira is Nigerian currency and that amount is slightly less than £400).

So she discussed her interest with the manager and they both agreed that it is more profitable for her to buy bags and sell, so she invested that small money and started her fledgling business promptly. She sells those bags very quickly to her church members and quickly words spread about her within the church. Considering the fact that her church members are more than 20,000 strong, her business grew rapidly from there on. Lately, her single order was in excess of £20,000 from the lowly £400 initial capital. She now employs people to go out and sell the bags for her and she pays them commission. Let me put her case in context because if you are reading this in Europe or America you may wonder if her current status is a big deal but let me tell you, in a country where the annual salary of a teacher is £2,000 she has done very well indeed, and by the way she hasn't stopped. If she continues at this rate it won't be long before she achieves greater things in her life. The lesson here is that she starts with a little and gradually builds momentum towards independence by taking initiatives and the persistence to stay the course. I am more inspired by her story than some of my more affluent customers and I use her as example a lot when on the speaking circuit.

There is nowhere better to practise the idea of building momentum other than starting a business or starting any worthwhile endeavour. Starting a business is not when you put your goods or services on display for potential customers; it starts with the ideas occurring to you. When such ideas occur, the number one action to take is to write it down. Why is this important? This is the process of moving it from idea form into concrete form; this is a natural principle of manifesting your goals. You may be asking what if no idea occurs to me and I still would love to do business. I would ask you two questions:

What do you like to do and your eyes will light up just with the thoughts of doing it?

What are you good at doing? – The way to recognise this is when other people marvel at how you manage to be that good at doing so and so

Your answers to these two questions should be the hidden clue you have been searching for. Don't look for an extra-ordinary idea people have never done before. This may help you clarify what I am talking about. Who would have thought that Martha Stewart of US would make hundreds of millions dollars just by teaching people homemaking tips? You can turn anything into a business. If you have an idea and you want clarification on how to turn it into money, please visit my website *ayobenson.com* and leave a message for me. I will surely get back to you.

The lesson of momentum – small actions taken

consistently would build up enough energy to propel you towards your goal assuming you follow through on what you plan to do. Today, I will make it easy for you to be decisive, some people have more than one idea and they are conflicted as to which one is the best. This is the most common ground for procrastination. How do you bypass this stage? I will tell you about a simple method I got from the book *Tough Times Never Last but Tough People Do* by Robert Schuller. It is called '*Count to 10*'. When you encounter a challenge or a dilemma you must make a list of 10 possible solutions, don't overthink it just write them down and immediately start implementing the practical ones in your list. The first time I used it, I was amazed at how quickly my challenge was resolved and it helped me find the cash to pay for my Institute of Chartered Accountants of Nigeria (ICAN) exam and that's why I am in a position to communicate with you today.

Recap on what to do
- Write down all your ideas of business in your head
- Find one that you feel great passion for and pick it
- When you do this exercise, your gut will guide you so use it
- Write down your initial plan
- Take immediate action and schedule one small action to take daily for 7 days; what you are doing here is building momentum.

By day 7 you will be brimming with energy and you may not be able to stop even if you try to stop yourself.

"Most of life is routine - dull and grubby, but routine is the momentum that keeps a man going. If you wait for inspiration you'll be standing on the corner after the parade is a mile down the street." - Ben Nicholas

I like Ben Nicholas' analogy of life as a parade, you don't enjoy the parade if you stand in a corner to wait for inspiration on how to join in; you just jump in and have fun with other people. Some people think routine is boring but to accomplish anything in life if you don't get into a sort of routine of doing it you may never accomplish anything. Cristiano Ronaldo is the best player in the world but he does more than 1000 sit-up exercise daily. What a boring routine, some people may say but there is nothing routine about his ability and bank balance! Repetition is the first law of learning and the more you do something the better you become and the better the result you get!

As I have noted at the beginning of this chapter, the easiest way to build momentum is to start an endeavour and if you apply this knowledge in any goal you want to achieve then you are half-way there! It is more difficult to be in the zone of indecision and the moment you decide, you get the energy to move faster as you build momentum. Having built momentum, you will be like a moving train which starts slowly but when it gets going, it would crush anything in its path! So build your momentum and be a moving train, then you will be unstoppable!

What would you start today that you have been thinking about? Start it now and the universe will support you! Start Now!

CHAPTER 11

PEOPLE:
The Pillar of Progress

"First-rate people hire first-rate people; second-rate people hire third-rate people"
- Leo Calvin Rosten (1908 – 1977, American humourist in the fields of scriptwriting, story writing, journalism and Yiddish lexicography

You have no doubt heard the phrase *'no man is an island'* countless times. This is so reflective of whatever you do in life. Nowhere is this truer than when you venture into business. You cannot run a business without getting other people involved. This is not a lesson on human resources management but an insight into finding the right people for the right position in your business.

Qualification is very important, but then it should not be the only basis for employing people – there is more to a person than the qualifications he or she is wielding. It was said that interviewers know whether or not a candidate would get a job within the first 30 seconds of meeting them. Well, I don't know if that's completely true or not but what that suggests is that the decision is somehow subjective and disregards all the efforts to formalise the process into a logical assessment of the candidates. It is false economy to look for people who will take the least amount of wages on offer because it has been said that if you pay peanuts you will hire a monkey! Instead look for winners and they would make you the money to pay their higher demands if you manage them well.

As a manager, the most important skill to develop is that of hiring the right people and it is true in life as it is in business. I use analogies relating to sporting activities a lot because it is similar to business and when they say art mirrors life and vice versa it is very true. In any team sport, the most important personality is the coach as he is the driver of the team and the most important part of the coach's job is hiring the right kind of talent to blend into a winning team. John Wooden who won 12 championships as a coach at UCLA and one of the most respected minds of his era once said that there is no secret to success in sport; it is the art of getting the right kind of players and then getting the best out of them individually and as a team. In football, the Barcelona team that achieved phenomenal success as at the time of writing this book is full of unbelievable talents, even when their erstwhile manager, Pep Guardiola, who was the inspirational leader, left the club they continue to dominate and win trophies.

If you set time aside to find the right kind of talent for

your business then you are on the right path to success. You are probably convinced now that it is critical to find the right kind of talent for your business. If you are like me, you should be asking how you would go about this difficult task. Let me share with you some of my ideas of getting to know people at a deeper level to help you judge if they are right for your business or not when hiring. There is a truism that has been ascribed to various authors, but which nonetheless holds a certain actuality: 'Tell me how a man eats and I would tell you his character'. The truth to this concept is that the way people do small things is the way they do big things; that is the first thing to bear in mind. Secondly, you must know that human beings are a product of habit, so the way you live from hour to hour would determine the level of your outcome. When people are coming for interviews they are very prepared for technical questions at least the diligent ones; you may not get as much information to help you make an informed decision. Knowing people at a deeper level involves asking questions about mundane day to day stuffs.

My approach is to ask all the technical questions first so that at least I am sure whether the person is capable of doing the job or not. Then you gradually dig deeper into their personalities. You have to be careful in arranging your questions in such a way that it doesn't cross the line that may cause offence or be outright illegal in terms of employment laws in your country. Let us assume that you are looking for someone who is outgoing, gregarious and influential (these are some of the qualities of a good salesperson). If you ask them directly, they probably would tell you straight away that they have all those qualities even when they don't! There are clues to differentiating between extroverts and introverts and really some people are just right down the middle and you may design your questions around those clues. If you are looking for a salesperson you need an extrovert who is usually energised when around people, he loves to talk and is very outgoing as part of his natural make up. The clues are: they talk a lot; they have a lot of friends, they are open and approachable and they solve problems by talking about it. You may observe some of these clues as you interview the candidate but a note of warning is that some people maybe extroverted in certain situations and be introverted in others! Ask them if they have a lot of friends. If they do, probably that's an extrovert.

Another way to decipher someone's character is to ask them how they spend their typical day from the time they wake up till the time they go to bed. This is one question that has been very useful for me in understanding how people spend their time, how organised they are, how they relate to people, sometimes you may get to know their belief system or you may get to know their values etc. Sometimes you ask people why they study their course and this may give you an idea of their hidden motivation. I once asked a candidate who studied Applied Physics but applied for Marketing Manager Position and he said growing up he was so determined to change the world and he thought the course would be the route towards doing that! I hired him and he was fantastic and doubled sales for us in the first one month and a lot of growth afterwards. There is no proof that introverts can't be good salespersons because if you combine the conscientiousness of an introvert with the ability to influence you may have a good salesperson but my own conclusion is that people's natural ability must be explored and employed rather than trying to improve on areas where they struggle.

You must not base your judgement on a single factor in making decisions to employ, but rather a combination of factors to ensure that you reach a decision that you feel is right in your gut. There is a psychometric test called DISC which measures four key important aspects of our behaviours: **D**ecisiveness, **I**nfluence, **S**tability and **C**autiousness. This test is free and it is available online. I won't be going into the details of how it works but it has been greatly useful to me. My candidates are very grateful for taking the test because apart from helping us know them, they also have a useful tool from the result which helps their self-awareness; so they may capitalise on their strength.

Getting the right people for your business is very important as this is your opportunity to harness the strength of many like-minded individuals towards the achievement of your goals. My final admonition to you is that if you found a great candidate please don't lose them because of wages and I have said this before! We will cover in another chapter some negotiation tactics you may adopt in everyday business situation to help you win more as this is required in many areas of business. Negotiate with your candidate if their demand is outrageous as long as you feel they would deliver for you.

"I hire people brighter than me and then I get out of their way"
- Lee Iacocca

Let this be at the back of your mind: that you must hire people that are brighter than you and then squeeze every ounce of productivity out of them. Your business would leap above competitors who hire average people.

CHAPTER 12

The Art of Selling

"Ninety percent of selling is conviction, and 10 per cent is persuasion"
- Shiv Khera, Indian activist and author of self-help books

Selling is as old as commerce and you will be surprised that the method used hasn't changed that much for thousands of years for people getting average result. The world has changed but methods and principles used remain simple and obvious. My favourite musician is Will.i.am and he is the most maverick of an individual. You get to know people more when you observe them in action. On the BBC musical talent hunt programme, **The Voice**, he has become an enigma well loved by the viewers. What I observe about him is that he does the opposite of what you expect him to do and sometimes I feel a sense of disappointment at him for that, but if you look at his career, that's his makeup and he has been extraordinarily successful.

My point is that if you follow the crowd, you will get average result! But dare to think outside the box; do the opposite of what everyone else is doing, you will get a result and whatever the outcome, it does not matter as long as you learn from it and continue pursuing your goals. Okay, I digress sometimes so, let's come back to the art of selling. (Mr. Selling) hasn't got a great reputation in the consciousness of most people and for obvious reasons! When you learn that someone is coming to sell something to you; you may subconsciously put up your guard initially until you are convinced it could be something useful to you. No one likes to be sold! If you are in business you have to sell whether people like it or not, so what is the solution? My rule is IF YOU WANT TO SELL, DON'T SELL! Paradox? If you are wondering what it means, please just take it literally, yes I said 'don't sell'. The less you seem to be selling to the public or individual the better and I would explain to you how to go about it. Before I delve into the details of how to sell without selling, let's review the story of one of boxing's most flamboyant characters. The name Don King generates all kind of emotions and probably expletives from certain quarters, don't worry about the person, just learn from his method. This guy is the ultimate seller and he doesn't sell directly, look at his appearance and tell me who dresses like that for goodness sake! The hairstyle standing straight looking into the heavens and outrageous costumes the Pharaohs would have been proud of.

Everything about this man smells selling and you wouldn't even know it. I am a follower of boxing, if you ask me to name a promoter that comes to my mind first; it's going to be Don King. Well, don't get me wrong, I am not saying that you should dress like a Pharaoh to go and meet your bank manager otherwise the men in white coats would come and take you away for good measure. I am telling you about his appearance because it is not by accident that he dresses that way; it is part of his indirect selling method. This man was born into poverty and developed the hustler mentality and got himself involve in illegal betting rackets to finance his University education. He eventually drops out of the University to focus on his gambling business. His life turned dark when he beat someone to death for whatever reason but was acquitted of murder charge; he was however convicted of manslaughter.

In 1971, he was paroled and now a free man he decided to go into the boxing business. How do you get into the boxing business? It is like any other business - so you do what every other business does! Register a company, hire employees, raise money, start small with low level boxers, grow organically and one day, may be one day there would be a chance to get the professional boxers on your team after years of toil. That's what you and I would have done. Okay then, that's why we are not Don King and of course I don't want to be but I want to get better at selling! He thinks that if he goes to the big boxers and say I have just started this promotional company and please allow me to organise a big boxing match for you; what do you think they would say to him?

GO TO HELL! This is what direct selling does to your aspiration. So the cunning man that he is pursues a different route. He wanted to raise money for a charity (Cleveland Hospital) and the best way to do it in a meaningful way is to organise a boxing match. Who in the world is the boxer he could have approached? Mohammed Ali! What?! Yes, he got his wish and the boxing bout was extremely successful. That was his opportunity to prove his ability and he took it with both hands. From that moment on his career was launched and the rest is history as they say.

He circumvented like twenty years of hard graft by a simple method of indirect selling and he started from the top and remained there. Whatever you say about the man, you must give him one credit, he is extremely savvy in business. So let's come back to our indirect selling method you can apply in your business on daily basis. It doesn't have to be as dramatic as the story but if you bear in mind that direct selling is not as effective as soft indirect selling then you start thinking about the approaches you could adopt along that line. Some examples of how to sell successfully albeit indirectly are discussed in subsequent chapters. You don't have to agree with everything I say but I will advise picking the examples that align with your values and implement them immediately.

"If you are not willing to risk the unusual, you will have to settle for the ordinary" - Jim Rohn

Create events

"The true sign of intelligence is not knowledge but imagination."
- Albert Einstein

People love events and that's why the sports franchises engender strong emotion from people and it is the reason why 60,000 people will gather at Emirate Stadium to watch an Arsenal match in London. Imagine that the ticket for Arsenal is one of the most expensive in UK yet people get themselves ready on a Saturday sometimes with their spouses and children and pay over the odds to be part of the event. Can you get people to feel this strong emotion about your business? If you imagine the inconvenience associated with attending a match especially when it is not in a glamorous stadium as the Emirate then you will realise the power of events on people. Well Arsenal FC is the club I support so excuse my bias if you spot any!

Another example of the powers of event is the one associated with religions and there is no more mass patronage in the world bigger than emotions generated by events associated with religion. The story of the success of MacDonald was actually associated with the understanding of the power of events and building the selling strategy around it. At the beginning of the rise of the company, the strategy they adopt is to site their outlets close to a big church so that when people close from the church there is ready meal waiting at the MacDonald outlet for them. Did the strategy work? You don't need any evidence to tell you that it was a spectacular success.

Sport enthusiasts, congregation members, club members etc. have one thing in common, they enjoy events and the rituals associated with them. How can I use this to help my business you may ask? You can create events about anything you want and the examples are all around you. I am going to show you one of the easiest ways to create events is to launch a company or a product and make it entertaining. Now you have to be careful not to waste a lot of money doing this and when you do make sure the event pays for itself. I am not going to give you the details of how to organise the event or the event to organise because the environment and culture of your area will determine the most effective events for your company. Individuals may use events to promote themselves too and it follows the same rules. I will give you a skeletal outline of the structure of your launch to give you dramatic effect.

Giving back to the community is one of the most effective ways to do a launch and the example readily comes to mind of Don King raising money for a charitable cause to get his career off the ground. For the benefit of our current generation, I can give you an example of a Hip-hop artist that used exactly the same method to advance his career. You are unlikely not to have heard the name *P. Diddy* before? Whether or not you follow the urban culture, you must have heard about this enigma of a man. His real name is Sean Combs and since that's not edgy or cool enough in the hip-hop world, he first adopted the name *Puff Daddy* and then changed it to P. Diddy (whatever that means!)

I have read about his meteoric rise in the world of entertainment and my conclusion is that this is another man who doesn't follow the crowd. When P Diddy was 22, he was largely unknown and still trying to get his career off the ground. He organised an event, I repeat, he organised an event! This event was meant to raise money for AIDS charities and many rap stars were invited to come and play basketball. The event was named *Heavy D and Puff Daddy Celebrity Charity Basketball Game* at City College's Nat Holman Gymnasium. To cut a long story short, this event ended in tragedy as nine people lost their lives and several were injured. That was a sad outcome. The number of people that attended was much more than the 2,730 capacity of the venue, so they probably underestimated the potential response to the event. People were desperate to get into the venue and they feared being left out as they quickly realised that the capacity was much smaller than the crowd outside waiting to get in. How would you like a crowd of people to be in such frenzy about your company or yourself? You know the answer; organise an event. P. Diddy was devastated by the outcome but the event launched his career as someone capable of attracting a lot of interest and as a credible promoter of events. A little note is that this young man was in the University and dropped out to pursue what he loves most i.e. music and it pays off for him. So event can make the huge difference as part of your selling strategy regardless of your environment. P. Diddy is on top of his game and he is worth hundreds of millions of dollars and he keeps going stronger and stronger on the strength of that initiative to organise an event for charity. There are strong emotional triggers you must notice here: the power of celebrity, the power of sports, the power of altruism, and the power of events; when you mix the four attributes then you expect 3,000 people for an event but you get 12,000 instead, so when you are planning your events expect the unexpected and be prepared.

The event must not be about you or your product but make sure your name or product name feature prominently in the promotional activities; that is how you get the most mileage from organising such events. You will turn people off if you overtly promote your product and the event may lose its appeal. So be clever in the way you plant your brand subliminally in the minds of people.

Create a community
When people are in a community they tend to behave in line with the direction of the community; so you may direct your community to behave in a way that helps your business and also helps them. You cannot take without giving, that's a powerful guiding principle if you want to remain in business for the long term. Culture evolves from this idea that people in the same community do things in a peculiar way that differentiates them from

other communities; therefore the tendency is for people in that community or at least, the majority to follow the direction of the community.

In my community in the south-western part of Nigeria; there is the entrenched culture of respect for older people which is not found in any other culture in Nigeria. The language actually sets the rule of how you address an older person differently from the way you address your colleagues. For example, if I am addressing someone next door and you cannot see the person, you will know whether that individual is older than me or not if you understand the *Yoruba* language. When I speak English you will not know whether the person I am speaking to is older than me or not if I was in another room where you cannot see us! The reason is that it doesn't matter in the context of the English culture so it isn't necessary. So back to creating community; interaction is the key to creating a community for your business. I studied a case study on eBay while I was doing my Masters of Business Administration at Oxford and I realised that the reason why people are so engaged with the auction business model is the non-stop interactions between customers. From listing your product until it's closed, there is good engagement with the punters. Even after the sales, there is still room for interaction and the feedback system is also a powerful tool that contributes to the success of the company. So eBay has created a community albeit unintentionally and their brand is now a worldwide phenomenon. There is so much opportunity to engage the customers, and with the social media providing instantaneous two-way communication between you and your prospects, you are advised to use it to good effect. You can find resources online on how to engage your community so I would not necessarily go into the details of that on this page. If you do this very well, you will have an army of enthusiasts that are not only your customers but your advocates. This way, selling comes off as a piece of cake rather than a struggle.

You may organise your community to interact with each other regularly by creating discussion points around their interests as well as the interests of your immediate community. If you do this well, it would come to a time when the community would take it over from you and manage it directly themselves. Check out the community on *eBay*, *Amazon*, *Yahoo* etc.

You must invest some time in learning the social media rules; this is what would give you the edge over other competitors. If you have the resources to hire someone who is knowledgeable in this area, it may give you a very good mileage in achieving your selling objectives. However, I must warn you that the rules change very rapidly and what works well a few months back may no longer work now, so you must keep up with the changing rules and exploit it to your best advantage.

The Power of Authority

Selling is all about influence and if you are perceived to be in a position of authority by your customers, they tend to listen and follow your direction. This is why people follow religious leaders without question and it's as powerful as it is dangerous. I have heard about some charismatic religious leaders that hold such influence and power over their congregations that they would not question whatever the leader asks them to do including sometimes killing themselves! This example is all around us in this day and age; as controversial as that may sound, the human mind can be easily influenced and it's not as difficult as you might think. Now use this knowledge for good and not for evil because you may accomplish both with ease using this concept. How can you apply this in business? Richard Branson is the authority in the use of this concept and he has managed to build an empire using it. He is able to command investment from people effortlessly like no other entrepreneur. In his book *Business Laid Bare*, he talks about dialling for dollars to take over the then Northern Rock Bank failing business and the money we are talking about is in billions; when you move from selling your products successfully to selling ideas then you become the superstar entrepreneur like Richard. He has built this power of authority since the beginning of his business adventure. He is never shy of putting his name and personality out there in support of his business. He is one of a kind in terms of his ability to generate interests and get massive followings for either his companies or products. Be known to be an authority in a particular area especially in the business that you are engaged in and you will find it so easy to sell whatever it is that you are selling; products or ideas.

Chet Holmes is the master at using this concept in a practicable way to generate a lot of sales. In order to apply this method, he advises that you should find a problem the product you are selling solves and then design a training program around that subject and teach it to your clients. He advises that you must ensure that you deliver value in teaching your potential clients this method. In the process you must cleverly include the product or service you provide as one of the solutions to the problem they are trying to solve. He used this method himself with an out-of-this-world result of doubling sales and quadrupling of sales in less than one year. I have applied this in practical terms in my business and it works if you have the discipline to follow through as it is not necessarily an overnight success strategy.

Have a plan on how to present yourself as the authority in your area of business or even area of interest, your power to influence people will rise astronomically and you may get a lot of people to do your bidding. If you sell a product or service, then your job is made even easier! One way to build your authority is through the media. Engage the media and put yourself out there; make contribution to the community by impacting knowledge and helping people in the process.

Know Your Customer

This sounds like an obvious advice and you will be amazed at how many people just sell to their customers and they don't build relationship which is key to long-term prospect of their business. There is this notion that customers would only buy from the cheapest seller of products; that cannot be further from the truth. The most important duty of the entrepreneur is to build a long-term, enduring relationship with their customers. The first step in doing so is to interact with the customer and be deliberate about gathering information about the customer that would help you make important decisions on targeting the customer with the most appropriate offer. Big businesses are now very keen about knowing their customer on a deeper level than previously thought possible. Use of technology is one way of achieving this monumental task if you are a very big company. *Tesco* builds an unbelievable database of its customers by giving them a plastic card from where they gather a treasure trove of data about the customers, their spending habit, their preferences etc. It got so sophisticated that it was said they can predict when you are likely to come into the shop and which shop and what you are likely to buy etc.

Gathering information about your customer is very easy these days. With the social media and technology apparatus that you may use to analyse the data, this will most likely give you an edge over your competitors. When we first started in my business, I know the names of the top 10% of our customers and I speak to them regularly to build a strong relationship. This group of customer are like our advocates and they have a sense of belonging and feel as part of the business. We usually get loads of referrals through these people.

Reciprocity

I want to tell you a story to illustrate this point so that you will get the idea of how powerful the concept is. It is a personal story of reciprocity and embarrassment. It was a long time ago and it was 14th of February. If you haven't guessed what happens on that date every year, I would tell you it is Valentine day! I am not good at remembering dates, anniversaries and things like that and the stereotype is that men are not usually as adept at keeping track of such events as women. I cannot say that I am not aware because the noise about it is everywhere and it is a day lovers exchange gifts and remind themselves how wonderful they are (whether or not that's true!)

So it was a particularly busy day for me and by the time I got around to buying a gift for my girlfriend the shops have closed. Well, I couldn't even find a card relevant for the day. So I went home hoping that she too wouldn't buy me any presents and we may just go out and have a meal to just celebrate. You probably would have guessed that it is very unlikely that a woman would be as forgetful for a day like that! Ding dong, the doorbell to my house rings and see who is there with bags full of wrapped stuffs. I let her in and to my utmost embarrassment she brought out five different gifts neatly wrapped with lovely messages on each of them; accompanying the gift is a large card in a red envelop saying wonderful things about me. Honestly, if you have given me the chance to pay five times for a gift at that point in time, I would have been eternally grateful to do so! I couldn't lie to her so I just confessed and apologise that I would make it up to her which I did at five times the cost of what I could have bought her. She was very gracious about it though and I was extremely grateful for her understanding. This is the law of reciprocity at play here because in life you don't want to get without giving and it is enormously embarrassing if you, like me found yourself in this kind of situation. How can you use this concept to wow your customers and compel them to give back to you by patronising your product or services? If you give them something upfront then you are likely to get them to give back to you through their loyalty to your brand. What can you give that wouldn't dent your bank balance, it doesn't have to be expensive; for instance giving educational information about your products even before offering them for sale is a very cheap way to give to your customers in advance.

You may not believe how easy it is to give something back to your customers. Regular useful information about your product is an easy way to give back to your customers. If the regular information is very useful they would look forward to it and reward you with patronage and loyalty provided you do deliver on your promise to them.

The Newsletter – Your 20,000 Powerful Foot Soldiers

How would you like to send out 20,000 powerful foot soldiers to go and fight for your sales? Well it is within your reach, but not without some work to be in that great position. Before the Internet, the use of *Sales Letter* is very common and some people still use it today. I still get loads of Sales Letters, brochures, magazines etc. on daily basis. With the Internet, the game has changed, it is a lot cheaper to run newsletter and get through to your customers with the messages you want to pass through to them. The first hurdle is to avoid getting involved in that most hated word 'spam' because you don't want to associate your company or your person with sending spam to people so you must be sure that your lists are gathered carefully and truthfully. What is a list? These are visitors to your websites who left their emails to be contacted by you. Most customers would not mind being contacted and they willingly leave their email addresses with you for that purpose; however, some of them need to be coaxed, wooed and persuaded to accept being on your list. So you may ask: how do I go about doing that. Well, there are methods you may adopt to ensure you get the people to leave their emails. This is not a topic on how to gather a list but I would just give you brief pointers and then you go and find out more about it. Depending on the kind of business you are engaged in, you must give your customers the opportunity to register in order to get a gift. Those gifts are usually associated with an educational product 'how to do things.' For example as an author, if my community is mainly entrepreneurs, I may offer to give them my free audio recording of *'How to use newsletter to get loads of sales.'*

People want free things and it doesn't have to be big and you will be amazed at the level of interest you may generate when you offer a gift of any kind to your customers. I would tell you in later chapter how this idea of giving free gift has skyrocketed our sales especially when we just started the business. Having got the list, your communication must be savvy because you may lose your list as quickly as you gathered them if you are not clever with the use of newsletter in promoting your business.

Use of the headline
This is the most important part of your newsletter and it determines whether your recipient would open your newsletter or not. Use headlines that grab attention of your customers because this makes a difference as to the success or failure of your campaign. There are a lot of resources on how to write effective headlines, so you may adopt what is relevant to your industry. I can give you three quick tips on writing headlines which may help you get your newsletters opened by your prospects. Business is about solving problems for customers that they cannot solve themselves; therefore you must identify the

problem your customers are most concerned about and use it as part of your headline. Since you now know that I am an advocate of indirect selling, when you write your headline, you must address the problem you have identified asking questions about how to solve the problem. This may involve you doing a little research on how to solve the problem and you have the biggest resource in the world in the palm of your hand –Google! I would tell you an interesting story about my daughter, it is a very short one and it corroborates what I have just told you about finding resources online. My daughter is a teenager but she is not your typical teenager aged 13, but with the maturity of a 25-year-old. She is self-motivated and bright. One day, she asked me for money and she rarely does as she gets everything she wants from home. So, without asking her any question, I gave her £10 and I went out. I have taught her everything she knows from cooking, ironing, knotting ties and so on. To my surprise when I walked back in the evening she asked me if I would like to eat cupcake; I asked where did you get that from? She answered with a wry smile and said: "Dad I made the cupcake and it is delicious."

I wasn't quite sure what to make of it because I have never made a cupcake myself and I am not big on cakes, chocolate and other processed, sugar laden-stuffs. "So who taught you how to make cupcake?" She looked at me with a surprise look on her face and she said, "On YouTube, of course." Out of curiosity, I tasted one and it was really delicious. If a 13year-old knows where to find information to make cupcake then you too can find information on anything you want to learn. So back to newsletter, go and find information on how to help your customer solve their immediate problem even if it doesn't sell your product instantaneously, it would mark you out as a person or business that cares about his community and the goodwill alone is worth more than money. There is this psychological saying that the one asking the question is the one in charge or in control, so when you ask your customers questions you are bound to get a response verbally, mentally or in writing in response to your question. When you write your headline or subject, make sure you incorporate the question that addresses the concern of the customer and you would enhance the probability that your newsletter would be opened. Address the customer in your headline as 'you' make sure it is all about the customer not how great your product or company is in your headline.

The body of your newsletter
Use a lot of visuals in the body of your newsletter to illustrate your point. Offer solution to the problems of the customers that you have identified and then call them to action; which means you must tell them what you want them to do after reading your newsletter e.g. shop now, click here, register now etc. There are a lot of companies offering newsletter services and where do you find them? You know the answer already! Google!

I used to work in Advertising as a Finance Manager

but I learn all areas of businesses where I work and this is a sure way to get an edge in life. Our Managing Director at the time is a genius when it comes to writing effective and successful copy. So there are rules you may apply to give you structure when you write your newsletter copy.

In this day and age when information comes at us from various angles via multiple devices, it is a lot more difficult to grab the attention of the reader. The number one rule is to make sure that you write in a way to get attention of the reader, especially your headline. Try different ways of saying the same thing and rank what's likely to get your attention if you are the reader! You may also get your colleagues to assess the suitability of your copy to generate the desired result.

Interest - You must know your target audience so that you may include what is of interest to them in order to keep them reading. So when you have determined the interest of your audience, choose copy that would keep them reading. What is of interest to teenagers may be a turn-off for middle age people!

Desire - If you get attention and address the interest of your audience, they still need a reason to buy your product or service; therefore you must package your communication such that the audience wants what you are selling.

Action - what action do you want your audience to take? Buy now, shop now, register now, download now etc. You must give specific instruction to your audience exactly what you want them to do.

Beliefs

> *"If you don't change your beliefs, your life will be like this forever. Is that good news?"*
> - W. Somerset Maugham

Do you believe in what you are selling? There is this common saying among salespeople and they would go '*I can sell ice to Eskimos.*' An Eskimos' life is ice; they live ice, eat ice and sleep ice, so they don't need ice! This translates that I can sell anything to anyone whether they need it or not! I don't think this is a healthy concept or belief. When you believe in what you are selling and you know what you are selling is beneficial to the people buying it, then you are in a better frame of mind to sell it in large quantity. I don't want to make judgement about what other people are doing to make money but those making tons of money from products that bring nothing to the universe but harm would get their payback one way or another!

So I would say to you my friends: sell something useful to the community and by all means don't sell ice to Eskimos! Belief is very powerful and it is at the root of every great thing that has ever been done in the world as well as the most heinous of crimes in the history of mankind. Why this is relevant at all in the art of selling is that you must have the belief that you will succeed in this endeavour to have any chance of success. A belief is just your thoughts that you keep thinking and the good news is that you can change it in a moment. Our thoughts should not just happen to us, it is important that we take control of it and direct it towards what we want rather than allow it to just happen! We can only hold one thought in our mind at a given time, the way to direct our thoughts towards what we want is through deliberate repetition of the thoughts we want; so go and practice and see what difference it makes to your life. If you have done a good job of your indirect selling, and you believe in what you are selling then influencing your prospect becomes so much easier.

Believe in yourself - There is a mental component to every action we take in life and belief plays a great role in whether we undertake a task at all, let alone succeeding in doing it. This is even more important in the game of selling because you need to believe in yourself first and foremost: in order to influence another person to take any action and selling is not an exception.

Self-confidence comes to some people naturally and they don't have to cultivate it! However, if you haven't got it you can cultivate it very easily by changing your view about yourself. Our view of the world is unique to us and at short notice and with a little help we may decide to change it and therefore change our lives. Teachers have a great role in shaping the future of kids and my school experience was a typical example. It takes an inexperienced but charismatic teacher just a few first hours of lesson to change my view of the world. The general belief in my school as I started secondary school is that the subject mathematics is the most hated and difficult of all subjects and most students don't do well in it. So we all believe it and no one wants to make the effort to learn it. Then two years into my secondary school, this teacher arrives and guess what subject he is teaching; mathematics. This was a young man on the mandatory National Youth Service Corps (NYSC) scheme at our school and I have never had so much fun in a classroom as I did at his first lesson. My love for mathematics started on that day and I ended up becoming a Chartered Accountant. My life would have been completely different if one teacher doesn't only change my view of a subject but causes me to fall in love with it. What is it that you feel is difficult and you need to fall in love with that may change the course of your life for better? My teacher changed what my belief system zoned in to be difficult at that time to something that I would consider to be fun! If you sell then you must believe selling is fun, you must believe challenge is fun and derive satisfaction from every move you make in the process. My fun subject prior to my new teacher's magic was history and I still love it and I scored A1 in it which is the highest grade available at the time for my School Certificate.

Maybe I would have become a history professor which is great but perhaps I wouldn't have done all the fun stuff I am doing now as an entrepreneur. Can we all be lucky to get a charismatic teacher to change our view of the world? Probably not! It actually doesn't have to be so because you can change your view of the world yourself in a heartbeat. How do you do this without help? It is a simple method of passing the message to your subconscious mind. Repetition, repetition and repetition of the belief you want over and over again. Alternatively, a more powerful way is to change your personal history and this is one of Richard Bandler's discovery which has helped a lot of people live better and more fulfilling lives because it is so effective. I have used it to get rid of a lot of childhood emotional baggage which otherwise could have stalled my progress towards achieving my dream. The process is simple, you just write down the new belief you want and then imagine that from childhood you have always had that belief and put your imagination to use in adopting this belief as you go through life to date. You may have to do this a few times until it becomes part of your personal history. You can also use this method to delete the negative beliefs you no longer want as if you have never experienced it!

What kind of belief do you need to be able to sell? You must believe what you are selling is beneficial to your customers and this is the most critical belief because it would motivate you to keep going when there is a little challenge along the way. You must believe that selling is fun and it is something to look forward to! Have the belief that you are capable of influencing anyone as part of your natural make up. Have the belief that you are capable of accomplishing anything you set your mind to achieve.

Belief is very important in our lives and we cannot do anything except we believe we can and that includes selling!

Overcoming Objection

Whatever you sell, there is always an objection. The more value you give, the more likely people are suspicious of you on the surface of it; it is your responsibility to ensure that you bypass the objections and positively influence your prospect. Some entrepreneurs think that the best way to compete is to lower their price thereby lowering their margin and making their business a lot less profitable. We did this experiment in my business, whenever we have a new product, we conduct price testing. This is where we take the 2 similar items not exactly the same but with the same landing cost and we put one at a lower price and the other at a higher price; the one at the higher price sells quicker because it is not what something is worth, it is what people think it's worth that matters! The difference between intrinsic value and perceived value may be very different depending on the product and the positioning of the product! Price is usually not the only objection you need to address, there are myriads of them; if you know your product or service well it is very easy to identify possible objections such that you may address the issues upfront as part of your message to your customers.

Let's talk about price now. Pricing is more of a perception than measure of value! I buy a designer perfume from a regular shop for £50 but this same perfume is sold at Harrods at £500! Does it make any sense to you? It's all about the perception of the buyer and the power of branding. When you sell something more expensive than the substitute you need to adapt your communication to bring out that innate tendency in people to associate high price with high value! You must address the issue before the customer does because that way when he thinks of high price he associates it with high value. Don't present your talk as a hard sell because your customer may see through it; but make your point in a passing conversation discussing the product. You may say something along the line of some people are unaware that nothing is cheap for nothing and may opt for cheaper option but at the end of the day, they would pay more as cheaper products will not deliver the same quality as this one!

You may do this for quality, time, terms etc. The important thing to note is that you are aware of the potential objections your customers may raise and address it in advance. Make sure you also emphasise to the customers that they are getting a good deal even after close of the transaction so that when they get home they don't feel like they have been ripped off.

Overcoming objections may be relevant in other areas of your life and you use the same approach to emphasise the opposite of the objection! The rule is that you must attach good feelings to the product you are selling even after the close, in order for people to keep feeling that way 'ever after'! When they feel good about what they have bought then they would not only come back to you but they would introduce loads of people to you. Do you want that or not? Then overcome objections and make your selling process a fun one for you and your customers.

The Power of Influence

Selling is all about influencing people to behave in a certain way that favours you or other people. Some people think it is very difficult to influence people but it isn't really so if you know what to do. People like those who are like them at the subconscious level and there are many ways to show them that you are like them without making it obvious. When you meet a stranger for the first time, you may have certain level of suspicion no matter how small until the person interacts with you and if the experience is pleasant then you may start to think that you can trust the `individual'. Dr. Milton Erickson is the genius that established how to influence people from the subconscious using hypnosis and self-hypnosis!

Imagine being unwell in your hospital room as a teenager and you are overhearing three doctors discussing with your parents that you will be dead by the morning! What kind of emotion would you feel and what would you do? I bet you are unlikely to say *'I was damned if I would die without seeing one more sunset. If I had any skill in drawing, I could still sketch that sunset.*' This is the response of Dr. Milton Erickson on his sick bed diagnosed with polio! He survived of course and was one of the top psychiatrists of his era, helping people resolve some of the most difficult psychological and psychiatry problems considered hopeless cases by other therapists! Erickson asked his mother to reposition his bed so that he may view the sunset. The combination of his desire and anger that the doctors had the audacity to tell his parents their child was going to die in the morning was his motivation for staying alive; according to his own account of the incident. The universe has a way of preserving the lives of those that are likely to cause a great change in the world. When doctors make unpleasant prediction about you or family member, remember that they are not God and that their opinion is not necessarily final! So back to the process of influencing people before digressing into the story of Dr. Erickson. It is now a common knowledge that the way to influence people is by forming rapport with them at the beginning of the first encounter. The most useful of his teaching is that words are not enough to influence people as he observes that someone may say something verbally but his entire body language may say something completely different. He has been extremely successful in his therapy work by using the clients' non-verbal cues to cure long standing illnesses and phobias. How do you translate this knowledge into influencing people in your selling activities? A skeletal outline of the method will be made available here and you may go away and research more into mastering your communication and your ability to influence people.

There are several ways of building rapport with people and one of them is to find a common ground very quickly and it may be anything like hobbies, movies, politics, weather, sports, holiday destinations etc. You may know this already but do you deliberately use them to build rapport with your clients? In selling, building relationship is very important especially if you sell directly to customers and gathering information about your customers is a very good way to do so. Another means of building rapport is through exploiting the subconscious mind by a method called matching! When you match the sitting position and mirror someone's posture, you are telling that individual at the subconscious level that you are just like them, it's very simple to do and the other party will not even know it. You may also breathe at the same rate as the individual and that's even more powerful. I must warn you that there is more to this concept than I have just described; it is much more powerful and you may find resources on this subject by studying some of Richard Bandler and John Grinders work on Neuro-Linguistic-Programming. This is a simple way to build rapport with your prospect in order to increase your chances of success. This concept is not just useful in selling but also useful in building good relationship with your friends, family and acquaintances. Communication is the most powerful resource we have as humans and it is the basis of civilisation and all the great things yet to be accomplished by mankind. Spend some time mastering your communication and there is nothing you cannot do; selling is just a small part of the infinite possibilities available to us as an effective communicator.

The use of words in communication remains a potent means of exchanging ideas, though people may say something and mean something else; if you are adept at listening you will be able to pick out the verbal meanings and the non-verbal meaning of words and interpret them to work for you. Some people use visual images in their communication and it helps them understand if you use visual language in your communication with them; you would be able to influence them more readily than using other modes. The same goes for those who prefer the auditory mode; when you communicate with them in the same auditory mode they are likely to understand you better and it is easier to influence them. I haven't got enough space to do justice to this method here but you may study NLP further to gain more understanding of the method.

Timing

In my experience of running seminars and conducting experiment on human behaviour, many people are habitual procrastinators and you find them in every walk of life. Sometimes, it cuts across all races and backgrounds; hesitation is a very common problem for a lot of people. In selling, you may have convinced someone that they need to buy; also they might have decided to buy, then they stall and postpone taking the action necessary. They are not being difficult, that's just the way they make decisions! How can you help them overcome this problem so that you motivate them to decide on buying your product or taking the action you want? Give them a timeframe! Now! Buy Now! Register Now! Download Now! Have you encounter any of these recently, it is issuing a timeframe for you to take certain actions and it works. So when you communicate, let your prospect know that the time to take the decision is now! If now is not practicable then give a specific timeframe and withdraw the offer at the expiration of the timeframe.

Don't use this method
I observe this selling method and it is quite effective, but I don't recommend that you use it. However, if it's been used on you then you must recognise it and bail out! I called this method overwhelm and confuse the customer! This is common where there are no price list and you have to negotiate the price and what you pay depends on your negotiation ability. May I say this is common in Nigeria where most sellers don't display their prices and you have to hone your haggling skills to get the best value. When you enter a shop and four or five assistants welcome you and they overwhelm you with information and confuse you as to what you actually set out to buy! If the buyer is not savvy enough, you may end up buying

something you don't want at a price way above necessary and bag load of buyer's remorse! This is not a good strategy for long-term relationships because the buyer would be unhappy afterwards, they would neither come back nor recommends someone else to you. Now, that's not how to build a long-term business. So don't use this method!

Deliver good value

Selling does not end when you get the money and this is a short sighted view of business. To get the benefit of a long-term relationship with your customers, you must sell them what they want, at the price that is reasonable and also follow up to ensure that they are happy with their purchase. The number one rule of selling is that you must know your products in and out! Those selling from their shops sometimes have salespersons that are smartly dressed but they have no idea how the products work! This is not good for the customer because they need to understand that what they are buying is the right thing for them at that point in time. Knowing what the customer wants, advising them on the pros and cons of a particular choice would build your credibility and you will avoid buyers' remorse. We would discuss the issue of buyer's remorse later.

Close

You must know when the customer is ready to make a decision to buy and at this point you must close. Some people continue selling after the customers have already made the decision to buy; that's not good because you may actually undo the good work you have done and the customer may still change his mind if you keep going after they have made the decision to buy. So ask question to test when the customer is ready to commit and close at this point.

Beware of Buyers' Remorse

Have you bought something before you got home and feel bad for buying it? That's buyer's remorse and it happens to people all the time. Why should you care if your customer has buyer's remorse after all you have been paid? Well the reason is they won't come back to you next time and they would not refer customers to you. So you must ensure that your customer is happy with their purchase and that they have bought exactly what they want. If you do the steps above very well, you will prevent buyer's remorse. Ensure that you understand exactly what the customers want and be sure that's what you sell to them. Allow your customer to return goods if they change their minds. There is a company in the United States (Zappos) who build a billion-dollar company in less than 5 years by adopting this method; they give their customers 365days to return their goods if they change their mind. That's not the only thing they do, they also have excellent customer service. Now, it would surprise you to hear that this company does not spend any money on adverts, they believe that the advert budget would be focussed on pleasing the customer and it works! Find a way you can wow your customer and they would be loyal to you. Follow up on the customer after the sales to be sure that they are happy.

This is the longest chapter in this book. Yet, there isn't enough space to exhaust everything about selling but if you apply what you have learned here and cultivate the desire to know more, then you are on your way to succeeding in your selling activities and as a result expand your business both in the short and long term.

CHAPTER 13

Conquer fear!

"An absence of fear of the future and of veneration for the past. One who fears the future, who fears failure, limits his activities. Failure is only the opportunity more intelligently to begin again. There is no disgrace in honest failure; there is disgrace in fearing to fail. What is past is useful only as it suggests ways and means for progress."
- Henry Ford (1863 - 1947, American entrepreneur and founder of Ford Motor Company)

We tend to dismiss the life of animals in the wild as chaotic, brutal and crude; we think they have no culture, no communication, and no order! This view cannot be further from the truth. I salute those who have the patience to look at the lives of animals in details over a period of time to understand their survival instinct and their way of life. You may start to wonder; what is animal life got to do with you? Nothing, except the lessons we may learn from a specie that doesn't generate a lot of emotion from people but have a fascinating, well-organised community and impressive governance that puts the human race to shame.

This animal is a ferocious hunter and its hierarchy in the wild is not that great but they use team work and fearlessness to get their ways against more formidable powerhouses of the wild like lions and leopards. They mark their territory and guard it jealously within their community and if an intruder ventures into this territory they devour it mercilessly including their own specie. You may jump to the conclusion that this is so cruel but if you look at humans, we behave exactly the same way.

I have watched elections in Europe recently and the manner in which some politicians tear into immigrants as worthless benefit-seeking opportunists is no different from these wild animals I am talking about! The cheetah is a carnivorous animal and they are organised into communities. They sometimes allow others into their community if they prove due loyalty and obedience to the hierarchy.

In this fascinating community, the females are usually the alpha leader and the social status of the female ranks a lot higher than the male and there is strict rule about observing this social status when it comes to order, sharing of resources including mating partners. The female is bigger and stronger; however, this social status arrangement is never questioned and it is enforced with brutality when challenged.

In the world of humans, how do you get your social status up in our society? It may not be with the primitive brutality of the animal world but it is equally brutal in its own way especially getting to the top and remaining there! You have to rule by intelligence rather than the strength and size of your muscles. However, understanding the fact that nothing in the world would be handed to you on a platter is the beginning of the path to progress. If you want an improved social status, then you must be prepared to fight for it physically, mentally and spiritually. The reason for telling you about this animal is not their governance or their lifestyle; it is because of their ferocious hunting ability and opportunism. This is where I want you to understand that as it is in the animal world, so it is in our own world and we can observe to learn a great deal from it!

The female leader controls everything and the first child is the heir to her throne automatically and no one challenges it. From the time the child is born if it is a female, she starts getting preferential and deferential treatment from the whole community and its social status is only next to the matriarch! To simplify their governance, it is just similar to the British monarchy! How preposterous is that? How can animal evolve and design such sophisticated governance system? I already warned you that they are much more than we think of them!

Cheetahs hunt like a well organised army and no prey is too big for them to confront; that's not even their most impressive characteristic! A very big hyena just killed a big giraffe and it pulls it under the tree and because of the sudden speed and energy just expended, it must wait for its temperature to cool a little before eating otherwise it would just pass out! That is a big mistake when cheetahs are about; I haven't told you what their most impressive characteristic is yet, it is fearlessness! They are the most opportunistic hunter in the wild and they eat everything including the bone discarded by other wasteful hunters! So the hyena lies on its belly watching its meal and salivating; cannot wait to eat properly after days of hunger! Here come the cheetahs! About fourteen (14) of them descended upon the meal like a swarm of bees. The hyena is bigger and stronger and would not have any of that nonsense; so it fights back the cheetahs! The cheetahs would not bulge, they would fight for it and they are more in number so as the hyena attacks one about five are biting him behind with ferocious intensity. The intelligent thing for the hyena to do is to abandon the kill and make a dash for his life. He who dares win! The cheetahs do this to other bigger, stronger and ferocious hunters; so they haven't got the fear gene in them at all and they rarely go hungry or better put, they are always hungry! Are you hungry? Are you as hungry as the cheetah? When you are hungry, you are driven because you have an immediate need to satisfy! You don't have the time to wait; you just pounce just like the cheetah! When you see a hyena guarding its meal, are you as hungry enough as the cheetah to strengthen your powers by attacking in groups?

Are you fearless? Are you as fearless as a cheetah? Would you move without hesitation? Would you find the courage to break down walls or jump over it or tunnel underneath to reach your goals?

Let's break it down! Hunger is your obsessive desire to get to your goals! Being fearless is your courage to move without hesitation and without regard for perceived dangers! Attacking in groups is organising a mastermind i.e. like-minded people to plan with and execute your strategy. Chasing the hyena away is removing obstacles in your way! Eating the meal is enjoying the fruits of your labour having achieved your goals! When next you encounter an obstacle, remember this story and be a cheetah!

Be Hungry - Be Fearless - Be Smart - Be a Cheetah!

CHAPTER 14

Communication

"Take advantage of every opportunity to practice your communication skills so that when important occasions arise, you will have the gift, the style, the sharpness, the clarity, and the emotions to affect other people"
- *Jim Rohn* (1930 - 2009), American entrepreneur, author and motivational speaker

My workshop for my staff on building relationship with the customers is the most important workshop that we do for new staff. When my staff have difficulty with customers at the early stage of our business, they call me to speak to the customer. Some customers are difficult because of the way they see things, but you can make them see it differently and they would become your best friend. Our view of the world is unique to us and as long as we hold certain views close to our heart, we sometimes hold rigidly to that position. It is easy to cultivate and hold a particular position but it is also easy to change or realign that position with other people's view.

Now, when I have the task of dealing with difficult

customers that my staff have been unable to manage; I speak to them for maximum of five minutes and they would be laughing and joking with me, telling me about their personal life, their problems and their aspirations etc. So I ask my staff to call the customer back to conclude the transaction and they marvel at the turnaround; someone that was spitting fire a few minutes ago is now calm, understanding and happy, yet nothing regarding the transaction has changed! As we grow bigger, it is difficult for me to keep intervening in this manner and the best thing for me to do is to teach my staff how to manage the customers the same way or they could actually do it better than me because they would introduce their own method; it's all about the principle.

I have studied Neuro Linguistic Programming (NLP) for some time now and it has opened my eyes to some of the subtle idiosyncrasies of the human mind. So, I look out for those little things that may make a big difference in people and what I have found is so profound that I would share some of them with you.

I was watching the Graham Norton talk show on BBC in London one Friday evening. It is a chat program that interviews celebrities in a light-hearted format and engages an interactive studio audience. Well, you have got to laugh in life, so I indulge sometimes in programs that make me laugh, it is therapeutic! The actor Jamie Dornan who played Christian Grey in the movie adaptation of the bestselling novel, *50 Shades of Grey* is on the show but it was before the film was even made. He was probably there to promote some other movies and I picked something quite profound during the show. This narration may not be a verbatim representation of the event but the substance of the story is true. Norton asks him about the 'walk' and he burst into laughter and explains that he is self-conscious about the way he walks; he says that he walks on his toes in a bouncy kind of way so he demonstrates and the place erupted in laughter. He has tried so many ways to change it without success; he practises some other adaptation of the 'walk' with the help of his wife but still without success. So he describes how he went for an audition one day and the script says he should walk from one end to the other which he readily obliges. The director of the movie then asked him surprised at the way he walks: "Is that part of the act?" i.e. the bouncy walk! No he replied: "That's how I walk" and the audience burst into laughter at his demonstration. He explains to the director that he has tried to change the walk but without success! The director then says, why don't you land on the ball of your foot instead of your toes? That's it, the *ha ha* moment, he tries it and it works. Something he has been trying to change all his life was fixed with one phrase.

    I enjoyed the hilarity of the story but it also confirms my belief that words can change people in an instance; so if you believe this too then there is nothing about yourself that you cannot change and more importantly you will be able to help other people achieve the change they want just like the director helped Jamie change the way he walks, something he hasn't been able to do all his life. Why the story? I want to help you see the power of the spoken words and why you must develop your communication skills to achieve whatever you want.

Business is all about interacting with people and communication is the most feasible means of interaction whether spoken or written and this is what distinguishes humans from animals. Martin Luther King's speech '*I have a dream*' must have been played a million times; even generations yet unborn would play it again and again. It's not playing the speech that is important, it is what it represents and the change it has brought to the world. There are other profound earth-shaking speeches that turn the hand of history one way or the other and I want you to feel the impact of the spoken word and how it can move man to do the impossible. Team sports are quite difficult to manage because of the individual differences of the team members, their motivation levels are usually not the same, the relationship between team members may cause harm if not harmonious; sometimes, the management skills of the manager would also come to the fore especially when the team experiences difficulty during the season. I always used sports for my example because it is what I love and I observe it keenly to find what I can learn and then transfer it to the business environment. You will find out that there is a lot you can learn from activities unrelated to business which may be transferable to business and therefore get you unbelievable result.

So I am still talking about communication and there is no better environment where it is critical to master communication than football. A very good team without the right motivation may not achieve result because there are so many variables at play .e.g. injury to a key player, a player losing their head and getting sent off, a split moment lack of concentration, wrong decision by a player at a critical time, conceding unnecessary penalty, wrong decision by the referee which may swing the advantage to the opposition, etc. The list is endless. So, how do you communicate with your team to deal with any of these variables and still concentrate to win the game? Do you notice something similar to this in business? There are even more variables at play in business than in sport and if you are an entrepreneur I don't need to list them for you because you know them already. So how do you communicate with your employees to move them into action and still win the game of business despite all these variables?

When a football team is doing badly on the pitch, the commentators are usually talking about how the manager can't wait to get them into the dressing room to communicate to them what they need to do to change the course of the game. Well, when things are not going well in your business, are you eager to get your team together in order to redirect their focus through communication towards improvement that would make a difference and help you win the game of business? One of the most dramatic football matches I have watched and studied was the Manchester United against Bayern Munich in 1999. United were one goal behind at half-time and the then manager Sir Alex Ferguson addressed the team and he said: "If you lose this match, you will be about a few inches close to the cup while collecting your losers' medal and that in your career may be the closest you will ever come to the cup!"

Well, what the manager is doing here is to get them to feel the pain of losing before losing so that when they go out there in the second half those words would be ringing in their ears and when their legs are weary, the mind would be strong enough to move them. Tony Robbins, the American motivational speaker, personal finance instructor, life coach and self-help author, always talks about the fact that humans are motivated to avoid pain or to gain pleasure; he emphasises that using pain to motivate works better, because we are programmed to avoid pain at all cost. So we are prepared to go through pain now to avoid bigger pain later, so in your communication it is important that you find the pain that would motivate your team and direct their energy towards avoiding the pain in order to get the result you want them to produce. So back to the Manchester United match, they didn't score any goal until about five minutes to the end of the match. They went on to win the match one minute before the final whistle and emerged champions of Europe. They won the cup again about six years later and truly, most of those who played against the Bayern team were no longer playing for the Club; therefore the

Manager was right that if they didn't win it on the day they may never have won it in their career. Did the players think of it that way? No, it takes the ingenuity of the manager to tweak their mind in a way that stirs something which helped them win.

When I did my MBA, one of the most important modules is the one on leadership and communication. This is quite prominent in that we did a significant part of the course on communication! Listening goes beyond hearing what the other party is saying but you must also hear what is not being said that is, reading between the lines in order to make the right decision in those circumstances. Leaders must continually find ways to improve their communication skills; this is a kind of skill whose sharpening continues forever and you will be rewarded for those efforts as you will be able to accomplish more through your communication skills.

Management is not just about authority; it doesn't mean that employees would automatically follow you; you must find the right psychology and the right words to get the best out of them regardless of the challenges in their unique environment. You must continue to develop your communication skills throughout your life so that you may be in position to accomplish a lot of your heart desires.

CHAPTER 15

Negotiation

"You have to persuade yourself that you absolutely don't care what happens. If you don't care, you've won. I absolutely promise you, in every serious negotiation, the man or woman who doesn't care is going to win"
- Felix Dennis (1947 – 2014, English publisher, poet, spoken word performer and philanthropist)

Whether you are in business or not, every day of our life is a negotiation of one kind or the other. Imagine the ordinary day to day living if you have a family, it is a constant negotiation without necessarily calling it that name. The children want something or a condition that doesn't align with your schedule or values and you as a parent say no; well, don't you expect them to go away and accept your decision? No chance! Children are the most astute negotiator considering the fact that they don't have much power in the scheme of things, but they get their ways most times. My children have a well-practised negotiation method they use on me and I pretend not to know and sometimes you cannot just help but yield to them. This is a typical method they use: my youngest daughter is just ten, but she is the smartest and bravest of them all. She doesn't start her negotiation directly. She would go, "*Dad, you look tired let me get you a glass of water.*" So I know straightaway that a plot is brewing. "*Oh, thank you very much I can do with a glass of water.*" She finds the best glass in the house and brings the water. She would first sit beside me as I drink the water and you will think that's the end of it. I can see from the corner of my eyes the other kids giving her sign to make progress with their plot!

"*Dad, when are we going to Disney? Uncle is taking the twins to France in three weeks and we would love to go too.*"

"*You are still in school and we cannot go to Disney now and you know it*" I reply. They obviously know the answer to that question but since it is a plot I know very well so I play along with them. They start a conversation among themselves about a new animation movie that has just been released and how interesting their friends say it is! Since the conversation is between them I don't interfere deliberately, so I just watch the plot unfold.

"*Dad, today is Saturday and we are bored and we want to go somewhere with you*" says my youngest daughter.

"*If you are bored go get some books to read,*" I would say.

"*Dad, we have been reading all week and you know it. Why can't we go somewhere with you on a Saturday?*"

"*I am busy today as you can see but where do you want to go?*" They exchange glances and the word cinema pops out!

"*I don't have three hours to go and sit at the cinema today. I *have some work to do."*

That's the window they have waiting for and then they pounce!

"Okay, let's go to MacDonald's then; it shouldn't take more than one hour then we can come back on time for you to continue your work."

"You have been eating junk food a lot lately" I reply!

"Dad, you say we cannot go to Disney and we cannot go to cinema, at least we should be able to go to MacDonald's on a Saturday. Daaaad!" The whole plot is all about going to MacDonald's, they know very well that if they come with the 'can we go to Macdonald question', I would ask them if there is no good food they can eat at home; so they have structured the plot such that it isn't about eating, it is about going out with Dad. They have already lowered the stake from Disney to cinema then to Macdonald's; so this way I would think, well, I am getting off lightly when you compare the cost of going to Disney or going to cinema being much more than buying three Big Mac meals at Macdonald's. Now, I would have no choice than to take them to the fast food outlet, which is what they wanted anyway. Then I would say, *"Okay, let's go to Macdonald's then."*

Now that they have won, they would extract every extra advantage they can get out of me. "Dad, you are the best", one would say as we drive there, then they start conversation within themselves about the new meal at Macdonald's, how yummy the ice cream is etc. I want large says one to the other, I want large meal too and me too! They are testing to see how much they can spend!

To cut a long story short, children get their ways most times and the more you resist them the cleverer they become and you will have to yield to them. So children can conduct elaborate negotiation process; it is not as complicated as we think it is. The hindrance to our negotiation skill is getting our emotions involved about what is at stake. Children are not afraid of losing and they win more often than not. If you have children you will understand what is called 'pester power' this is why advertisers sometimes target children in their adverts because they know the moment children are on board; they would make the sales happen through pester power. So we are afraid of losing and like everything else in life, the moment you are afraid to lose you have lost! You must convince yourself that you don't care, that you can walk away from the deal. Having convinced yourself the other party will feel it in your attitude and you are more likely to succeed.

I have a question for you. Is negotiation a talent or a skill i.e. does it come to some people naturally or can it be learned?

Anytime I ask this question in a seminar I get the same answer, i.e. it could be a talent and it could also be learned. So that's very true. The only way to measure the effectiveness of your skill is the result you produce. Whatever skill that gets you result consistently has a structure to it, and most times the skilful individual may not even understand that there is a structure to what they do. There is a structure to negotiation based on the way people make decision on one hand and how the brain works on the other hand.

I would give you a quick story you can easily relate to as illustration of one of the key component of the structure of negotiation.

Who doesn't know John Legend, the legendary singer-songwriter and nine times Grammy award winner? Well I am not talking about his music today, I am talking about the lesson you can learn from this story but do enjoy the romance in the story as well.

In 2006, Teigen, who was a catalogue model at the time, was cast as Legend's love interest in the video for his single, "Stereo." She is a very beautiful girl of course but there are so many beautiful girls out there struggling to find a good relationship. She walked into John's dressing room and met him ironing his underwear and she was taken aback that a superstar of John's standing was ironing his own clothes, which was quite endearing, and she gave him a hug. After shooting the video the pair went back to his hotel room and she confessed that they hooked up. After that night she disappears deliberately and said she decided to give John some space so they didn't start dating until 2007 that was around one year after they first met. She says:

"I left him to be himself for a while. The worst thing you can do is try to lock someone like that down early on, then have them think, there's so much more out there. I played it cool for a long time. Never once did I ask, 'What are we?' Marriage was never

my goal, because I've never been very traditional. I was just happy to be with him."

In a nutshell, Teigen got her man and they eventually got married in a beautiful ceremony and guess who played at the wedding? Stevie Wonder! How cool is that?

What's this got to do with negotiation? I use this sort of story young people can relate to so that they will remember and they will apply the lessons. Have you heard the saying 'play hard to get' before, it is a simple psychology of human behaviour that whatever we want very badly, we cannot have! This concept has been around since the dawn of time but people don't have the courage to use it because of the fear of losing! Now what lessons can you learn from this story which could be applied in your negotiation?

Teigen didn't make herself available to John for more than a year, that's very patient and calculating of her; scarcity increases the value of anything whatever it is. In your negotiation it doesn't matter what the negotiation is about, apply the rule of scarcity and the value of whatever you are negotiating about will increase and if like Teigen you are at the centre of the negotiation then make yourself scarce. Every social encounter is a negotiation one way or the other so don't misconstrue negotiation as a strictly business affair. The word 'No' is a difficult one to say for most people because our culture teaches that we must be polite, considerate and generous. All of these are virtues but when in a negotiation please turn it off until your goal is achieved. I would tell you a personal story where 'no' paid off greatly for me and my company.

About six years ago my company was looking to buy a property in central London, it was at the time in London that the property market was on the floor and it's what you call the buyers' market. We were just being opportunistic because we have the cash and the interest rate was like 1% and I thought the crisis would not last forever and we have no immediate alternative use for the money. So, we get some agents to find a mid-range office property for us. There were a lot of them on the market, and there was this particular one that I liked on the edge of the city and I reckoned the price would skyrocket in no time after the crisis. The particular negotiation skills applied in this transaction is so simple and yet so effective that you will find it extremely useful. So we went there to look at this property owned by this research company so I asked them why they want to sell.

One of the most important aspects of negotiation is your ability to get the information which helps you determine your next move or helps you understand the state of mind of the other party. Questions are very powerful tools and you must learn to use it effectively. The answer to my question as to reason why they wanted to sell is like handing me a blank cheque and you will see why as the story unfolds.

They have just secured a bigger property outside London to cater for their expansion and they wanted to sell before moving to reduce their mortgage! Looking around, I see that there are a lot of boxes in place ready to be moved to the new location, this tells me they are tight for time – useful information. As a buyer, you must be alert to everything around you because they may present you with information with which to make the right decision. Some other people may not read any meaning to the packed boxes but because I have trained my mind to be alert to every stimulus when negotiating, it presents a very useful clue which helps my decision-making as the transaction progresses. I want to digress a little bit to entrench this concept in your mind. When I was a young kid, I joined the boys scout and there was this test that I found very useful up till today; they take a group of five of us and we enter an office and the leader sits at the opposite side and waits for about five minutes and then he asks how many chairs are in the office? He expects us to have noticed every details of what is in the room as we enter, so if you are just counting the chairs after he asks, you have failed the test. He expects that the moment you enter any environment you must take in everything in that environment and analyse it; according to him it may make a difference between life and death in a crisis situation. So if you practice this you will find it useful too.

Back to our original story; in a transaction involving high ticket items, time is usually critical in the whole decision-making process so let that sink into your mind. Time is the seller's enemy and if you are clever enough you may use this to your advantage. The longer it takes for the transaction to complete the more the pressure is on the seller. The reason why you hear 'buy now' is a psychological pressure on you so that the seller has an advantage the quicker you commit, so take your time. The seller would offer you a better deal if only you can keep him waiting. The seller wanted £1.3million for the property. A quick look would tell you they are about right considering the location, size and possible increase in value in the next few years! So I sent an offer of £800,000 to them! Preposterous? Not at all, what is the worst that could happen? They would say no! So they flatly refused the offer! You will think that's the end of the story. I (kind of) knew it wasn't! So we kept looking for alternatives and kept that property in view because I really liked it but I didn't call. I didn't even call my own agent either, because sometimes they work for both seller and buyer and make money both ways. So after three weeks, there was still no word from them. So I sent a clone to them, I would explain what a clone is, if you are buying a big ticket item if you are at a deadlock, you can send someone not directly linked to you to go and offer a price below yours and offer to transfer the money immediately as this helps you know the bottom price of the seller. Another lesson to learn is that information is critical in negotiation transactions as well as in real life. CIA, MI6, Mossad etc. are intelligence agencies with primary responsibility of gathering information about other countries and they spend billions annually on this exercise in peace time and in war. So sending a clone is like you own a little CIA to help you make the right decision.

My clone's offer was £750, 000 and he sent them a cheque with his offer! The next day, I got a call from them asking us to increase our offer for the deal. Of course, I increased it to £860,000 and we signed the deal and job done! Why go through all that trouble? Well, a novice would have paid £1.3million, so that trouble is worth £440,000 on a single transaction! The value of the property now is £2.5m and it is rising as new development are now going on around the area, it is now being branded the silicon valley of London as tech companies are now using the area as their base. So in business, you will do well if your negotiation skill is up to scratch, because apart from your core business, you will win in other key areas where negotiation is critical.

Let me quickly go through with you the lessons from the two stories. Scarcity improves the perceived value of an item, in the case of Teigen the wife of John Legend; it helps her get one of the most sought-after bachelors in the world. No bigger price and she applied only one rule, the rule of scarcity. Imagine yourself as John Legend, you can get any woman you want in the world or by the way every step you take there are women throwing themselves at you, would you pick any of those so easily available? Probably not! Then someone comes around, shows interest and disappears for one whole year, when next you see her, she would be worth more than gold, its simple psychology but most people haven't got the tenacity or courage to see it through! But you are unlikely to forget the lesson so use it!

In your negotiation, always remember that scarcity increases the value of whatever you sell; goods or services. You ask yourself the question: how can I present this product to seem as if it is scarce, and I would tell you some of the tricks. When you see things like time-bound offers, it is creating scarcity indirectly or you hear something like 'when it's gone it's gone' 'buy now' '3 days clearance sale' etc.

Big companies play this game with us all the time but we just don't recognize it. Have you ever seen the queue in Europe, US and indeed all over the world for Apple's products when they are launched? The perceived value of the products skyrockets as a result and they can charge any price they want. Another interesting observation of mine is that some restaurants in UK and US would not let you in except you have booked in advance, that's creating scarcity and the perceived value of dining in such restaurant goes up, not because of the quality of their food (they are usually decent though) or the service but it is a business model based on the scarcity sensibility.

How do you use this in direct negotiation? If you are very keen about a transaction and you show it, you will probably pay a lot more than you should. When in negotiation, you may use reverse psychology if you are the buyer, always have alternatives, and let your seller know that either directly or indirectly. Don't be too direct about it because your seller may also be aware that you are putting alternatives about to his face for effect and that way it may not be effective! Have you gone to view a property and there are three or four other people viewing it at the same time? They are indirectly creating a scarcity, it's a principle, it's a method; they are not there by accident and don't be surprised if some of them are clones as I already described to you earlier!

Another lesson to remember is that time is the seller's enemy so be patient, it would pay off. Then of course once in a while, you may lose out on a transaction because there is no certainty in this world but on average, you will be a lot better off if you apply this principle, the longer you keep the seller waiting the better your deal gets!

If you are buying a big ticket item, there is nothing tougher than finding out what the seller's real price is! Information is critical if you want to have an edge in a transaction. Open your eyes and ears for clues and you will find the information if you listen carefully and observe your environment as I already illustrated with the boys scout experience

You should be able to extract further lessons to learn from the 2 stories and add them to your own techniques or methodology.

We have only looked at a single step in the negotiation process.

I already discussed the fact that there is a structure to negotiation so we would look at the guiding principles you may apply and you have the choice of deciding what is appropriate for each circumstance to enhance your chance of success at negotiation.

Preparation - I have discussed importance of preparation in whatever we do in this book already, therefore this is not new to you so when you have to negotiate, be prepared! Musicians rehearse, dancers rehearse, sports people train, speakers prepare and you get the idea! To succeed at anything you must improve your skills; communication is an unending learning process so improve your communication skills and you will get better at negotiation

Left brain or right brain – if you have prepared very well, you must have found the right kind of emotion to stir in order to get people on your side. We think that we make decisions rationally at all times and that we cannot be swayed by emotions; men are more apt to think this way and these are the group that is most vulnerable to the pulling of the heartstring method. You will be amazed at how easy it is to get people on your side if you know what their trigger is.

Don't argue – what!? How can you not argue in a negotiation? Absolutely, you can. People will resist you when you argue with them and even if you win, it would be a pyrrhic victory because they would resent you afterwards. Instead, try and change their view of the world, their perception of reality and they would see your point of view the way you want them to.

Win – win approach – This is a good idea in an ideal world and if you are able to find the way for both parties to win, go for it. But in the real world, you must be going into a negotiation with the belief that you are going to win. Jose Mourinho's players said no matter how small or big the match they are playing, Jose wants them to win and he would prepare as thoroughly for the small games as he does for the big games. Jose's team rarely lose games and that's very rare in modern day football. If you go with the belief of wining you are more likely to win than go in with a doubt in your mind. Go into your negotiation thinking of winning and you are likely to win.

Alternatives – people can be fixated on a single outcome when negotiating but you must let the other party see alternatives that are better than their position or at least close to it. You will find this when you do your preparation, so arm yourself with it as it may be useful. You may also have an alternative that is even better for you too so, it is wise to explore this during your preparation. Be careful not to be focussed on just reaching an agreement, ensure you focus on your goals.

Body language - It has been said that 7% of our communication is words and the rest is about our body language, tone of voice, attitude, facial expressions etc. You must align your words with your body language such that you are congruent enough to be convincing. You can use emotions to buttress your point and this is part of your preparation. Let me tell you a method used by musicians to build and align their emotions with their body language during performance, it is not new and it's called the *mirror effect*. Practise your performance in the front of a mirror and watch your own body language and align it with your words. The top performers like *Beyonce*, *Will.i.am*, and *Kelly Rowland* have publicly said this, so I am not teaching anything new. Use it to your advantage.

Reputation – people are influenced by those they respect so maintain a good reputation. You must know that reputation is the perception of others about you not your intrinsic worth; so package yourself in a way that earns respect. Lawyers are adept at this as they put criminals in a shining suit and tie to present an aura of respectability regardless of their crime. So dress and look the part and you must also act in a consistent and fair manner or at least be seen to be doing so. You must also be personable even when you have to express your viewpoints in an assertive manner.

NO – I have discussed this before that people are not used to saying no, therefore if you want to win in a negotiation this is the word you must learn to say again and again. Some people call it walkaway point i.e. your deal breaker; this is a very important part of your negotiation weapon and if you look at the quote at the beginning of this topic it says:

"You have to persuade yourself that you absolutely don't care what happens. If you don't care, you've won. I absolutely promise you, in every serious negotiation, the man or woman who doesn't care is going to win." Felix Dennis

This is certainly not an exhaustive list of things you can do but if you apply the above ideas, your result should improve significantly. Negotiation is so important in business and that's why I have devoted a bit of time to it so make the most of the topic and do more research of your own. This doesn't mean you abandon what you have been doing but add the new ideas to your repertoire and you may win more than you lose. And when you lose find the lessons you can learn to help you win in future.

CHAPTER 16

Systems, Policies and Procedures

"Plan your work for today and every day, (and) then work your plan"
- Baroness Margaret Hilda Thatcher, LG, OM, PC, FRS (1925 – 2013, the Prime Minister of the United Kingdom from 1979 to 1990 and the Leader of the Conservative Party from 1975 to 1990)

I would like to welcome you to the exciting world of finance. *Yippee*! Yes, I am an accountant and there is this perception that if you choose the profession, you are a boring, grey suit-wearing, stiff, inflexible being interested only in juggling figures, systems and strange looking graphs! I think that's harsh, but I can understand people looking at us from outside may feel a little bit of that! Please don't skip this page thinking I am going to discuss figures or graphs. Far from it. I would like to show you one thing that could take your business from small to big, or from big to gigantic! It is the topic of this chapter; you must create systems, policies and procedures for everything you do from the beginning.

I said *from the beginning* deliberately because if you don't have this at the beginning of your business, it is a bit more difficult to implement when your staff are used to doing things haphazardly. It is easy for you to read this and agree that it is true but still not do anything about it, so I am going to show you two examples to crystallise it for you. I live both in Nigeria and UK, so my illustration will draw from my experience of both cultures. Nigeria is a country of great endowments too numerous to count, but after more than five decades of self-rule and determination we are still far from where we ought to be. But then, this is not a political book (though I intend to write one soon).

Back to the analogy that I wanted to show you. I love driving and actually I have no choice because that's the only means of commuting in Nigeria as I lived the early part of my life in Nigeria. How did I learn driving? I taught myself and don't ask me why - because there are no driving schools in Nigeria. Well, that's not completely true, but I can literally count the numbers of driving schools in Lagos with an estimated population of over 20 million people! So, you may ask where this story is going but just be patient and I promise you will enjoy it. By the way, why should I go to driving school if I am not going to take any practical test to get my licence, so no one does! It may shock people from the other parts of the world and they may view this with incredulity but it is true and I am particularly ashamed that we are running our country in this sort of way. So you apply for the licence and someone brings it to you at home if you are a big man or you go there to collect if you are less of a big man and money changes hand shamefully. This is just a background to my analogy so that you may see the reason why there is so much chaos, accidents and needless deaths on Nigerian roads.

I need to add though, that there are changes since taking place, but most processes are still characterised in the main by disorderliness. Corruption, once fully entrenched is endemic, a hydra-headed monster, perpetually rearing its ugly head at every twist and turn.

Now let's review this scenario and then imagine what kind of driving experience you are likely to have. You are not sure whether or not the next driver is actually capable of driving properly and you are on the same road, this would freak out some people in the West. At roundabouts, there are no rules, it is the rule of the most unruly which means those who are tough and bold enough to enter has the right of way! There are limited or no signs at all as to what is one-way, two-way or a no-entry road.

Policemen are known to stand at the end of one-way roads to collect bribe from unsuspecting drivers as the signs are quite obscure, too small or non-existent; I have encountered this a number of times and once I refused to give bribe, we would then drive back to the location for them to prove where the sign was. Eventually, they would let me off because there was none! Traffic lights are few and far between, and you obey the light when you feel like doing so. If you are in a hurry, it's free for all! Commercial vehicles are laws on to themselves and the number of dents on their vans is seen as badge of honour to warn other drivers of their boldness to engage their vehicles without the worry of getting hit! They stop in the middle of the road to pick up passengers and there is no law to deter them, well there is law to deter them but they can pay the police as little as the equivalent of a pound sterling to get away with it!

As a result of this lawlessness, you may be in the traffic for three hours for no reason at all because there are no effective systems in place to enforce order and decency. So, if you want to have a little of bit of laughter, come on a Nigerian road and view the absurdity of human existence. The only rule in existence is the rule of the loud horn. If you are in Nigeria for the first time, it is like an orchestra of deafening horn noise coming at you from various angles exasperatingly! This illustration is to show you an example of a state of chaos caused by lack of an effective system in place to regulate what people do and for something as important as driving, it becomes a daily nightmare for Nigerians commuting from one place to the other. The most appalling consequence of this state of things is that many lives are lost on Nigerian roads daily, there is no Nigerian that hasn't got a family or friend either maimed on the road or killed. One experience that I would never forget was a bus in a collision accident one early morning with about fourteen people on board with no survivors and the sight of blood on the road.

I hate to sound so gory but it affected me so much that I promised myself that, one day if I have the chance to express my disappointment at the state of driving in Nigeria, I would not hesitate to do it. Take a deep breath and let's look at the positives, sometimes an environment of no rules may feel exciting, you may feel giddy at the sheer absurdity of the whole environment but for something as important as the transport system, it is high time this was sorted out by the Nigerian authority.

Whenever I am in the UK, it is the complete opposite of the lawlessness in Nigeria. Don't get me wrong, traffic offences are committed daily in the UK but 99% of the time the rules work and they are followed because they are enforced. The reason for such orderliness is the understanding that when rules are made it must be enforced without fear or favour. Now this would be useful to you in your business, because when a Nigerian drives in UK they obey the laws and conform with the rules, so it's not the people apparently it is a matter of a dysfunctional system. When things work as they are supposed to do, then the positive outcome is inevitable. I have studied and implemented some of the Standards like ISO 9001, OHSAS 18001, ISO 14001 and their pivotal message is creating a system and adherence to the system which is the key matter but they also go further that you must always seek continual improvement on both fronts.

When you run a business where everyone knows what

to do and how to do it, you are half-way through the major cause of failures in business and you are likely to be on the path to success. The mechanics of actually creating a system is not rocket science as you need to have a system that is peculiar to the way your industry runs; as well as the uniqueness of your own business. In my business, we have systems for everything from monthly reports to filling generator with fuel so nothing is left to chance. Customer service follows a script and they have answers to all the possible questions customers may ask them, and if new ones come at them in the course of their work, they document it immediately and that's also part of the system. We then discuss the new question at our workshop and proffer the most appropriate response. Let me make it clear that our staffers do not read the script, they know it very well and they use their own style and language.

Even if you are a one-man business, please create a system for what you do still, and it will amaze you how it helps you get things done quicker and better. When you then employ others to run the business with you, it becomes a second nature such that your business may run like clockwork. I would love to make a list of everything you have to do, so that it may help you create a very good system, but I don't intend to bias you. So make a list that is unique to your business and start creating the systems, policies and procedures that would help you grow from being a small business to a bigger one in a short period of time. The point of the analogy is for you to judge how you want your business to run. The chaos on the Nigerian roads, or the orderliness of UK roads?

So if your business has no systems in place, you will experience chaos and no one gets result in a chaotic situation; because you cannot actually serve the customers well in such environment. However, if things are done in an orderly fashion, following pre-determined procedures designed to get good results, then you are well-placed to serve your customers well. When you serve your customers well, they would reward you with patronage and not only that, they would introduce you to other customers and sky is the limit for your business.

The world operates on orderliness, the sun rises every morning, and there is light and darkness at specific times. There are four seasons or two, depending on where you live, but it is fairly consistent. There is the law of gravity and there is growing and harvesting etc. So if the universe is made to order, then it suggests your business should be too and it would be able to serve and deliver the value for the community.

CHAPTER 17

Leadership

"People ask the difference between a leader and a boss. The leader leads, and the boss drives"
- Theodore Roosevelt (1858 – 1919,
American statesman, author, explorer, soldier,
naturalist, and reformer who served as the 26th
President of the United States

If you have read this far then it means you are a leader and you want to improve the way you do things and get better results. What is leadership? I am not going into definitions here but the key word in most definitions of leadership is *'influence'*. Influence who and how? The definitions suggest influencing people to strive enthusiastically towards the achievement of a group's objectives. You cannot force people to do things and get good result long-term; you may get short-term result but the human nature is such that they would rebel against coercion if it goes on for too long. This is why history is so unkind to most dictators. It is not any more difficult to inspire people into action than force them into action. So leaders who are willing to inspire their people would either have natural tendencies to do so, otherwise they would have to learn the art of leadership. Those naturally endowed also must find improvement in their methods; as in my view one of the traits of a good leader is the desire for non-stop learning about everything concerning their goals.

My own idea of leadership is that leadership starts from leading yourself! What does it mean to lead yourself? It means you take full responsibility for the state of your business and your life. When you are in business, you already have leadership foisted on you! Some leaders would blame everything around them when things aren't going right instead of looking at themselves analytically to see how things could be turned around. It has been said that if you don't admit you have a problem, you are no closer to solving it. I have observed the process of therapy for alcoholics and the first step towards treatment is for them to admit they are actually alcoholics and that it is a problem before any other action in the recovery process is taken! So as a leader you must take responsibility for the actions of your followers and the result of your business so that you may develop the clarity to proffer the right solution.

Do you have the courage to fire yourself from a job if you honestly analyse that you are not capable of doing it very well? I would tell you a story of Niall Quinn who was a fantastic football player in his days, he is also a good TV pundit; he knows the game inside out! One of the clubs he played for in his days was in deep financial trouble and needed urgent intervention. Niall takes it upon himself to lead a consortium to rescue the club and he pulls it off. He is now the Chairman of the club Sunderland FC. Most players' dream after their career is to become a football club manager and Niall is no exception and he jumped in to manage the club. To cut a long story short, the results are appalling and it seems the whole rescue attempt is about to collapse like a pack of card. What would Niall do in this kind of situation? He has so many options; blame the players, the referees, the finances, the pitch etc. He could easily have extricated himself as the key factor in the failure and look for a scapegoat. He fired himself and employed a manager and there is no shame in that at all. I believe that he examined himself and realised that he was not a good football manager; that's hard to admit but he was an honest man and I admired him for that.

Peter Ferdinand Drucker (1909 – 2005) is the Austrian-born American management consultant, educator, and author, whose writings contributed to the philosophical and practical foundations of the modern business corporation. His view is that you should find one thing you are good at and find a job where that thing is very important to be successful in life. Drucker states further that you may have all the weaknesses in the world, it wouldn't matter. People make the mistake of thinking that they have to be good at everything they try, you don't have to be; just find your strength and go for it. So Niall employs a fellow fiery Irishman in the person of Roy Keane. If you are not a follower of football, especially in

UK then a little dossier may help you understand this story. Roy Keane played for Manchester United and was the captain for many years. He is a strict disciplinarian and doesn't suffer fools gladly. The moment Roy takes over, the results transform immediately and Niall is now a genius in the eyes of the football world and in my book he is a genius indeed and an excellent leader.

The lesson I want you to learn from the story is not that the result turns out better at all; it is the courage required to analyse yourself honestly and come to the conclusion that is not publicly palatable and still go ahead to make the decision. The truth is that the result might not have changed for better and it would still have been a good decision made by Niall! Why? Such a leader would continue to find the right answers until he gets it right. One of the key aspects of leadership is self-awareness. How much do you know yourself? There are so many tools now available to help us look at ourselves critically and come to the conclusions that are sometimes more than 90% accurate. Some of us need this to understand our strength and therefore what it is that would give us the most value if we engage in it. I have done assessments like MBTI, Belbin, Insight, DISC etc. and if you type any of these in a search engine you may find some that are free and it would really help you dissect yourself critically and objectively to help your self-awareness.

Communication is another critical element of leadership and some people associate good communication with excellent grammar and use of fanciful words - far from it, and you will see why in a moment! This is common in my community where using big words is associated with how learned you are! As a leader, one of your strengths is the ability to communicate with your team to influence them to act collectively towards achieving certain group objectives. It doesn't matter what the nature of the goals you are trying to achieve is, it is paramount that you are capable of choosing the right words to move your clan into action. Leaders like Ghandi, King, Mandela, Lincoln and other greats have the power of words to such an extent that they are able to change the world just with their words.

I observe the power of communication as it propels two men from starkly different backgrounds and far apart continents to the highest position of power in their respective countries. Let me start with President Obama who was catapulted from an unknown Senator to the President of United States of America in a little over five years. One speech only did the magic and he connected with people in such a way that he etched his persona in the hearts and minds of most Americans. President Lincoln said '*I will prepare and someday my chance will come.*' Mr Obama was asked to speak at the Democrats Convention and he grabbed the chance with both hands and the rest they say is history. Was he prepared? Did his chance come? Did he grab it? If you want to be a leader, you need to devote some time in developing your communication skills.

Let me give you the story of another person who became a Prime Minister of Britain just as a result of one speech. It was like a mirror of the Obama phenomenon but it is even more ironic because of the conservatism of the British people. Surely, it should take more than one speech to catapult someone from obscurity in Britain to Prime Minister at such a young age; well it happened and the name is David Cameron. As at the time of researching this book, he is still the Prime Minister of Britain. Unlike Obama, David is from a privileged background and he gets a lot of stick for that, but why on earth that is viewed with disdain is beyond me as he had no hand whatsoever in the decision of who his parents are. I am not suggesting that this is how easy it is to reach such an exalted position and I am sure years of hard graft must have gone into developing their communication skills; you just need to recognize the power of communication when it comes to effective leadership. Develop your communication skills by reading, analysing, studying great communicators and you will not only succeed in business but any endeavour that requires influencing people; I don't think there is any significant endeavour where influencing people is not important.

If you are in denial about who is responsible for the result you get, it is hard to find the creative solution. Let me tell you a little secret that you must be aware of in business; stakeholders are in your business for themselves and they don't care a hoot about what happens to you. For example, the moment you are able to pay salaries to your employees when due they don't have any interest what happens to you or your company. I am saying this to you from experience as a business owner not as an author! If you have investors, as long as you pay dividends, they don't care what happens to you. Your suppliers love you as long as they get paid on time. Your debtors want to pay as late as possible for their own benefit and your creditors want to get paid immediately or at least when due.

Your only ally in this stakeholder business is your customer. Why? If you find a way to serve them well they would be your advocate, they would be loyal to you and your business would grow as a result. As a leader, to succeed in business make your customers your number one ally and you cannot go wrong. If you understand this fact you will promptly take responsibility for your business and carry your people along towards the sole objective of serving the customer to the best of your ability as a group. The reason why I exposed the motive of your stakeholders is to help you make them accountable and this is one task a leader must master.

Motivating Your Clan
Money doesn't always motivate and as a leader, you must understand this maxim and incorporate it in your reward system. Social-emotional support and a genuine demonstration of empathy often resonate better with most people. My staff can call me anytime to discuss personal issues and I would give that time because it may prevent some bigger challenges for the staff going

forward as well as for my company. People cannot perform at their best if they have niggling issues bothering their minds, so it is important that such matters are dealt with without delay. The truth of the matter is that the employees are sensible enough not to bring frivolous issues to me and it is great comfort for them to know that I am available to support them in times of need, so they don't abuse it.

Freedom
This is one of the most elusive concepts in human psyche and it is the most important to everyone whether they know it or not. Most entrepreneurs love their freedom and this is the primary reason they get themselves into business. The desire for freedom is not limited to entrepreneurs; your employees have this desire too. If you can find a way to incorporate some elements of flexibility into your work system it is a great motivator. Some people would rather earn less money and have more freedom and this doesn't mean less work would get done if you plan it well. Modern companies in the tech industry allow their staff a lot of freedom to decide many things about their work and productivity actually surpasses the traditional 9-to-5 culture. These companies have no dress code, there is a lot of freedom to plan their day, there is ample supply of food and drink and the camaraderie engendered by this culture helps them excel. Give your staff freedom but ensure they are accountable for their productivity.

Leadership and Learning
"He who would learn to fly one day must first learn to stand and walk and run and climb and dance; one cannot fly into flying."
- Friedrich Nietzsche, (1844 – 1900, German classical scholar, philosopher, and critic of culture, who became one of the most-influential of all modern thinkers)

To be a leader is to commit to lifelong learning and if you must achieve the status of a very good leader this is non-negotiable! Never in the history of mankind has learning been as readily available as today. All the knowledge accumulated since the beginning of time is now accessible to ordinary people at little or no cost via the internet. What is the acceptable excuse for not learning in today's world? If you don't like reading, there is audio and video online where you can learn everything there is to learn; the only obstacle to learning is you but if you want to be a leader you must be hungry to learn. You must also be able to stay one step ahead of others and the way to do this is to continually improve through learning. This is the secret of learning and I learned this from Tony Robbins; he said when you read an author's biography you start to think like them and 'as a man thinketh so is he'. If you want to transform very quickly go and access the minds of those great people by reading their biography; by so doing you are on your way. Maybe one day people will be reading your own biography to know what makes you tick, because if you stand on the shoulders of the greats, you are on your way to greatness too.

Types of Leadership Styles

I want to move away from academic treatise as much as possible because I want this to be accessible to most people so I would not go into any definitions of these styles but I would refer to them in a way that is easily understandable. Leadership by force as suggested is where you lay down strict rules that must be followed rigorously without question. Military regimes follow this type of leadership style and it suits them well because of the nature of their endeavour otherwise their goals of winning wars may not be accomplished any other way. There are other styles in direct contrast to the above like participative, coaching, compassionate etc. All of these seek to carry people along in the decision making process. Decisions made seek to benefit all parties concerned in a balanced considerate manner. As a leader, you must have a lot of tools in your box to deal with different kinds of situation and if you are in business, no two days are likely to be the same so you must be prepared to use the appropriate style where necessary. Leadership is like cooking, there are so many types of tools in the kitchen serving different purposes. There are so many ingredients to grind, mix, cut, stir, mash and cook. Some of the equipment in the kitchen are used for specific purposes some are used for two or more purposes, some are used interchangeably; some are used frequently and some are not used for a long time but when required, they are even critically important. I am a good cook so I know what I am talking about!

So in leadership, you have to use the right tools for the right situation. I don't use autocratic method often but there are situations where it is inevitable to use it especially where the action or inaction of one person could potentially affect many others negatively. When you have applied this method, do it fairly and let it be seen to be fair so that you don't alienate the staff involved or give others the perception that you don't care about the well-being of the staff. You cannot run a business without an element of disciplinary method. No matter how benevolent you are, some employees would want to test your patience sometimes not deliberately but you must be prepared to deal with this headlong. When you rebuke an employee please do it in a balanced way. Sir Alex Ferguson, was the legendary manager of Manchester United Football Club for more than two decades and there is this perception in the press that he was absolutely belligerent with out-of-line players but he explained that when he rebukes his players it is done in a fair and balanced way; something along the line (*'how dare you make such a silly mistake, you are better than that'*). Within that statement is the stick and the carrot follows immediately i.e. 'you are better than that' statement gives the player the assurance the manager still rates him highly despite that mistake.

Another rule about human beings is that some people would rather you just cut off their arms than be ridiculed in public, so don't humiliate your employees in the presence of their colleagues. There is a great deal of psychology about managing people and it is important that you have a bit of insight into human behaviour and motivation to get the best out of them.

Please note that this chapter is too small to deal exhaustively with the topic of leadership; you need to go away with two things from this chapter, i.e. learning must never stop for a leader and that the leader has at his disposal many tools and clever use of them would bring the right kind of result.

CHAPTER 18

The Question of Money and your Belief System

"The world we see that seems so insane is the result of a belief system that is not working. To perceive the world differently, we must be willing to change our belief system, let the past slip away, expand our sense of now, and dissolve the fear in our minds"
- William James (1842 – 1910, American philosopher and psychologist who also trained as a physician)

I was listening to the news one lovely evening and I heard that a horse earned £2 million in a year. I am not a follower of horseracing or anything but the news got my attention! My question to you is how much do you think you are worth? I would put the question differently, how much do you think you deserve? I want to talk about belief system and money to open your eyes to the fact that success is a state of mind; it is about your attitude to money. You may apply all the ideas you have read in this book and other books as well and still not get the result you want; if you don't understand this concept that your belief system is part of the reason why do you well or not!

This belief about money is in your subconscious mind and you learn the belief the same way you learn to walk. Most people don't even know what their belief about money is and I don't have the privilege to tell you what it is. You will know it yourself by your current net worth! If you find it easy to make money that's your clue about your belief system and please don't change it. If you struggle to make money and you do everything you know how to do and still you can't make ends meet, then examine your belief about money. Some people don't really want money or at least they don't want a lot of it; if that's you, it is okay because you are happy with your status. Those of you who desire to have money but don't, then you must change your belief system for you to succeed in this endeavour.

As I said earlier that we learn our money belief system just like we learn to walk. So, if your childhood experience was that of lack, you don't know any better and you may grow up to `believe that it is so difficult to make money. I am not suggesting that everyone that doesn't grow up in an affluent environment would have the same belief; not at all, some people would conclude in their minds that growing up was tough but they would change that and do better in life. Money is a matter of attitude and this is why rich people may lose all their money but gain it back within a short period of time;

because their belief about money makes them a magnet for money.

However, there are people who accidentally stumble on a large sum of money through lottery or sudden fame but without the right kind of belief about money; they tend to lose the money very quickly because they feel they don't deserve it subconsciously. Mike Tyson earned about $500 million in his career and was declared bankrupt at some point. He is a lovely bloke as I have listened to him a number of times on TV and he claims to be happy without all the money; maybe that's true! The lesson is that it doesn't matter whether you struggle to make the money or you fritter it away, what must change is your belief system about money. Evander Holyfield too earned about $200million in his career and ended up with nothing, absolutely nothing! It is a similar story to that of Tyson and he came on TV one day and was asked how he managed to throw all that money away; he said it was bad advice. Well, I don't think he has learned anything because he needs to take responsibility for that mistake for him not to repeat it in future. He is now too old to box but that doesn't mean he can't make the money again if he has the right kind of belief.

Now let's talk about the lottery. Many people have won the lottery and it transforms their lives and that of their family for good. There are some people however whose windfall was more of a curse than a blessing! In 2002, a young man won about £9.7 million in the UK lottery. His name is Michael Carroll and as of then, he was getting unemployment benefit (living allowance paid to jobless people) from the government. His rags-to-riches story didn't last very long at all. He spent the money on drugs, alcohol and prostitutes. He gave away most of the money to friends and family. This is the textbook example of someone who doesn't believe that he deserves the money. The problem is not about the drug and alcohol; it is simply a poverty-conscious mind-set. Eight years after the windfall, he was declared bankrupt. He became homeless at some point and would later work in a biscuit factory earning £204 per week. He claims to be happy with his current status, maybe that's true and you cannot argue with that! Tyson said the same thing about being happy with his current status, which is refreshing but I know what I would choose and perhaps any reasonable human being would rather have the freedom afforded by more resources than less!

So you have seen three classic examples of a poverty-conscious mind-set! Now let's examine an example of wealth consciousness. Donald Trump in his book *'Think Big'* talks about how he almost lost everything but gained it all back in billions of dollars. There is no magic, he knows that making money comes easy to him and he works very hard at everything he does. One phrase that I would never forget is this belief *'the harder I work the luckier I become.'* This is a classic example of wealth consciousness because he knows that whatever happens he would always have money! The hard work is incidental because there are millions of people working so hard today that live in utter poverty. So, it is more about your mind-set and the solution is easy i.e. change your mind-set about money if you ever want to attract money. I have so many other examples of rich people losing their money and gaining it back within a short period of time; if you look around you there are numerous such examples. By now, you are convinced that making money is about maintaining a healthy state of mind about money; the question is how you change your mind-set from poverty consciousness to wealth consciousness. I want to state at this point that making money is not a universal desire of everyone; so you can also have a change of mind set about that desire of yours in order to have it flow to you.

I heard this story about self-belief which I would share with you to illustrate this point. In India, young elephants have ropes on their necks and tied to stumps of small trees; when the young elephant tries to move, the rope stops it from moving beyond the length of the rope! This same elephant grows up to be very powerful and it could actually use its trunk to uproot bigger trees if it chooses to do so! The interesting thing is that because the elephant has been conditioned to think that it cannot escape when tied to that small stump; so it doesn't even try. The elephant doesn't recognise its own power because of the conditioning of his mind. So what conditioning have you been subjected to that you still carry with you as a limitation; you don't know your own ability. If you imagine that the elephant wouldn't even try is amazing! Do you know a lot of people who are like this? I do. I used to be one of them until I realised that I am powerful beyond measure; there is nothing I desire that I cannot achieve. The only limitation is that which we were conditioned to believe; right now such beliefs are shattered and shouldn't have any hold upon your life anymore. Sometimes the knowledge that you are capable as you have just uncovered in this chapter may be enough but for some people they need a little bit of help; this is where the idea of visualisation may help change your idea about yourself and expand your view of your capability.

The concept of visualisation is very popular in the self-help community as well as sports and entertainment. Most people do it without actually understanding the reason for it. The first time I encounter that concept was in the book by Napoleon Hill called *Think and Grow Rich*. He talks about sitting down to visualise what you want in terms of money and say the words to yourself. In my quest for understanding the reason why it works I stumbled on the fact that it is all about familiarity. I assumed that it works because it works for me but it doesn't work for everyone; I have taught the principles to friends and family and it is like a miracle for some people but for some others, nothing changes! So why is it about familiarity? The primary role of your brain is to keep you alive i.e. survival! Your brain pays attention to something new because that's where potentially there may be danger lurking; but things that are familiar are accepted to be safe. Let me give you an example, if you enter a room where your friends are waiting for you, your emotional state is very unlikely that of fear or suspicion. Let's assume you enter the wrong room full of strangers you have never seen before! It is likely that your adrenalin would kick in immediately to prepare you for a fight-or-flight response. I am not suggesting that you are afraid of strangers (there is no need to be) but because you are expecting to see familiar faces and instead you encounter a room full of strangers and their reaction are likely to be that of suspicion too. You certainly would be in a different state of mind. Your immediate reaction is likely that you will apologise and exit promptly.

Now familiarity is not necessarily about whether it is positive or negative; even when what we are familiar with is not what we want, changing it may prove a bit difficult. An American soldier Sgt Bowe Bergdahl who had been held hostage since 2009 was released through a negotiated process in 2014. He is no longer familiar with the life he left behind and it would take a gradual process of change to get him familiar with his old life again. His parents were not allowed to talk to him immediately or even see him because this may affect him adversely. So the theory of familiarity is real and this is why people love to remain within the circumstances of life they are familiar with. Earning £2 million a year would scare some people to death but if you look at it this way; are you more important to the universe than a horse? Yes, of course! So, why shouldn't you deserve that sort of money after all a horse earns that in a year! Visualisation, when done properly, familiarises your brain with the idea of wealth if that's what you are visualising. It is the idea of winning if you are an athlete, or great performance, if you are in entertainment. When you visualise, your brain now sees your new status as familiar and would no longer steer you away from actions which may produce this kind of result. I discovered that meditation helps clear your mind in such a way that your visualisation becomes a lot more effective and enjoyable. If you visualise and your mind is wandering from one current challenge to the other; you may not get the desired result quickly. The acceptance of meditation is growing rapidly in the West these days like everything else in the world, some people may never accept it; so if you are one of them; you may skip the next paragraph but if you are open-minded and willing to learn, it is very beneficial!

Meditation
Meditation is a means of transforming the mind. There are many types of meditations; they are techniques that encourage and develop concentration, clarity, emotional positivity, and a calm seeing of the true nature of things. By engaging with a particular meditation practice you learn the patterns and habits of your mind, and the practice offers a means to cultivate new, more positive ways of being. With regular work and patience, these nourishing, focused states of mind can deepen into profoundly peaceful and energised states of mind. Such experiences can have a transformative effect and can lead

to a new understanding of life. This book is not to teach meditation but since I have mentioned it I might as well tell you the basics.

When you sit down to meditate you need to set up your meditation posture in a way that is relaxed but upright, usually sitting on a cushion and probably cross-legged. If this is not easy you can sit kneeling or else in a chair. Then join fingers and thumbs together to make an 'A' of your fingers. A light bulb gives light by completing a circuit of positive and negative elements; you are doing exactly the same with your mind; lighting your mind by joining both hands in this manner. Then you close your eyes, relax, and tune in to how you are feeling. It is important to be sensitive to your experience. Focus on your breathing for a while and clear your mind; some teachers say you must count from 10 to 1 some 1 to 10 or any number of your choice; this is to focus your mind and remove distractions. Do your visualisation in this state. When you have finished, count 1 to 5, giving yourself positive suggestions as you come out of meditation. As I have said that this is not a book on meditation, but if you want to find out more, get *Silva Mind* online to learn much more than meditation i.e. so many ways to solve life problems are contained in their program which lasts around 16 hours. Some celebrities have used it to project their career to a new level but they would not admit it because they think it is controversial; I would rather be controversial and help other people than stay on the fence!

The number one thing to change is our belief system in order to change our life; whatever we want in life is ours for the taking only if we believe that we can have it!

"Sometimes all it takes to change a life is to decide which beliefs do not serve you and to literally change your mind about those beliefs."
- Joy Page (1924 – 2008, American actress best known for her role as the Bulgarian bride, *Annina Brandel* in the film *Casablanca*

CHAPTER 19

Time

"Yesterday's the past, tomorrow's the future, but today is a gift. That's why it's called the present"
- Bil Keane (1922 – 2011, American cartoonist most notable for his work on the long-running newspaper comic, **The Family Circus**)

Time is a great treasure second only to our mind and the thing about time as a resource is that it is finite i.e. it is not retrievable; once it's gone it's gone! I have spent a significant part of my life in education and I don't know if your experience is different from mine but all my methods for time management were learned after my education. Why should our school system ignore the most dangerous, expensive and self-destructive habit of all: time wasting? Procrastination and time-wasting are like an inseparable couple, where you find one the other is lurking! Today, I want to give you a tip on how to combat this seemingly harmless habit that could rob you of the chance to fulfil your potentials. It is not an exciting topic, you will not get the quotes to inspire you but some of the things I am going to tell you may be something you already know intellectually but still, you don't do them. This is not a message for young people alone and I am sure top managers would relate to what I am going to share but I would say to you that the discipline to implement them is key; otherwise it's a waste of time for you and me!

Let me start by telling you that it takes 21 days to form a new habit, the moment the habit is entrenched, your productivity will explode beyond your expectation. So, what I am sharing with you is something to practice for 21 days; after that you are on autopilot for higher productivity and one step closer to that goal of yours.

Plan your day the night before so that in the morning when you are super fresh and raring to go, the planning doesn't put the handbrake on your momentum.

Make a list – most people make lists daily, if you are one of those then well done. However, do you complete your list daily? When I have done this in seminars, about 20% would say they finish their list most days- nothing wrong with that! So when I dig deeper into how many tasks are on their list, it ranges from 7 to 50 or more! What's wrong with that is the psychological effect of not finishing your list which makes you feel unproductive and that's probably true. Your list must not be more than six a day considering that you are likely to be disrupted during the day.

I would also share with you the dangers of distraction i.e. unnecessary or unimportant distractions but for now let's focus on ensuring that you complete your list daily. Allocate time to your tasks and maintain the discipline to stay within the time limit. There is a theory that a task will use up the time you allocate to it, so be strict with your allocation of time to task.

Have a running list – here you may have as many as possible and from here you could pick out your daily list of six. Tick them off when you have finished them; there is also a psychological sense of achievement for doing so and you will be motivated to complete the rest. You may divide your list into a four quadrants where each quadrant covers *Projects, People, Goals* and *Priority* – this helps you cover all basics such that everything that should be under your radar remains in view otherwise, with the pressure of business some important things would just drop out of your consciousness and important things may not get done.

TYPICAL 4 QUADRANT PLANNING MODEL

PEOPLE	**PROJECTS**
People you are expecting things from	*Moving office*
People you are waiting on	*Launching a product*
People waiting for your response	*Implement a system*
GOALS/PRODUCTIVITY	**PRIORITY**
Sales	*Employ more salespersons*
Employees	*Buy motorbikes for delivery*
Customers	*Place advert in newspapers*

You can fit everything about your business in these 4 quadrants such that you have a full view of what is important and urgent; also keep in view things that are important but not urgent because these are the most neglected tasks of all and the omission of them may have serious consequences. An example of this is doing your tax return, it is important but not urgent; if it isn't in view you are likely to forget and this may cost you dearly!

People – You cannot do business without people therefore all those people whose help you need to get things done must be contacted regularly or at least when needed. There are times when you are expecting actions from other people; the problem with other people is that you are not their priority in the scheme of things therefore you are likely to go to the bottom of their list if you don't track them. This section gives you a view of all these people and you may have to remind them to take the actions you want them to take.

Projects – is a planned task that has a specific purpose and its time-bound. To succeed in business, turning tasks into a project would help you tackle them methodically and successfully by defining your goal and allocate resources to it and review at the end of the project. Typical examples of projects may be launching a product, implementing a system, moving office etc. So at every point in time you have all your projects in view so that you may allocate resources to them and ensure they also happen. Many people have good projects in their mind and they never get around to doing it, this would prevent such lost opportunity

Goals – This is an important part of business and it helps clarify what is important and you may be able to rank the goals and allocate resources to them. The mere fact that you see them daily is critical towards the achievement of your goals from psychological point of view.

Priority – Make a list of priorities and rank them under this section. This allows you to allocate resources to the most valuable task and this includes time allocation. Seeing your list of ranked priorities daily would help you focus on the most important task to embark upon.

Email - this is an important part of business these days that we cannot do without. As useful as it is, if you allow it to run your time, you will have no time to do anything else. Simple solution is to set a specific time for dealing with your email and stick to it. If your email alerts you for any new message, please turn it off except if your job is just to cover the emails only and nothing more. Still on email, when the subject of your email changes, ensure that you also change the subject and train all your staff to do the same. This gives you the chance to find emails relating to the subject matter when you need to. Let me give you an example, I write to my GM and the subject is 'My trip back to London' and he replies that all arrangements have been made but by the way the property agent sends the offer letter for you to sign and it's herewith attached. The subject remains ' My trip back to London' in a few weeks' time if I want to check the offer letter for any reason, it would waste a lot of my time because the subject should have changed to offer letter from the agent! You will see how little housekeeping like this could save you tons of time.

The concept of 'touch it once' means that if you have opened an email or a letter ensure that you deal with it immediately. If you do this it would save you a lot of time because the time you spend revisiting issues would be saved.

Big projects – if you don't have good time management skills you will find it difficult to start a big project. The trick is to break a big project into small chunks and allocate one hour of your day to attend to it. You will be amazed at the momentum you will generate and thus helping you achieve the goal. Big projects are important in business because that's how to achieve the big stuffs. Henry Ford accomplished a lot in his lifetime what may take others 10 lifetimes to achieve and I love this quote of his about big projects and you better like it too and use it!

"Nothing is particularly hard if you divide it into small jobs"
- Henry Ford

I will give you the rest of the steps and you may then research more on them.

Organise your folder on functional basis to allow easy filing and retrieval – this saves you a lot of time spent on looking for documents - ensure there is simple logic to your filing system

Delegation – My in-tray is always empty because if I cannot deal with it immediately I am delegating to a competent member of my staff. Learn to let go sometimes because you need to focus on what really requires your attention and what is also of productive value.

Do the most important task in the morning when your concentration and energy is still strong and fresh. A note of warning, I am a morning person but others may be night owl; where they do their best work in the middle of the night so you must know when you are at your best. Doing your important tasks when you are most alert is one of the most critical success factors.

The 20-Minute Rule – Humans can concentrate at optimum level for only 20 minutes without any break. If you break your concentration every five minutes when dealing with an important task, then you are unlikely to be productive because each time you are interrupted, you will have to go back to the beginning of the concentration loop. To be effective, stay on course with your important task by switching off your phone, close your office door or instruct your staff not to disturb you for that period.

Telephone – another useful tool but it is also a timewaster if you allow it. Switch it off or put it on silence- this is not easy to do but trust me, nothing will happen during that period that you cannot deal with after your task is completed.

Prioritise – It's not all tasks that's important, there is a rule for prioritisation. When you encounter a task, ask the following questions and act accordingly.
Important and Urgent – Do it now 1st priority
Important and not urgent – Do it next 2nd priority
Not important but urgent – 3rd priority
Not important Not urgent – throw it in the bin! It's a time waster!

MENTAL MANAGEMENT

"Mental strength is really important because you either win or lose in your mind. And I'm not solely talking about sporting matches, boxing events - anything you do, you do it first with your mental strength. And you can actually train and develop it, and I am responsible for what I'm saying because I have experience with that."

- Wladimir Klitschko (Ukrainian professional boxer and the Heavyweight World Champion (2015), holding the WBA, IBF, WBO, IBO and recognised by boxing publication *The Ring* as its world heavyweight champion.

Having talked about time management and all the methods to improve, most people reading this book may know some or all of the above suggestions but cannot muster enough energy to implement it. This is why I would like to talk about mental management so that you would not only know what to do but also be mentally strong enough to implement it. I have been talking about alignment of the body and mind because it is an inseparable combination therefore productivity must take account of both for success.

How many hours do you work in a week? If you an entrepreneur, the chances are you are working from 50 hours to 70 hours a week and some much more than that! The secret of success in business is to actually enjoy the process of creating wealth and working excessive hours would take the fun out of it. Have you heard the saying that it is the journey that matters not the destination. It is inevitable that you may sometimes have to put in more hours when there is a project at hand that requires personal attention but the warning is not to make it a routine. There are simple things you may do to manage your mental state to help you follow all the good suggestions I have already given in this chapter.

Is Sleep for Wimps?

Physical and mental well-being is very important if we are to excel in whatever we do and there are some simple tips to help you maintain this state. Margaret Thatcher was the one who popularise the concept of getting more out the day by not sleeping enough and many professionals take the advice to heart and the consequences can be serious for health and wellbeing. She said *'sleep is for wimps'* because she sleeps for less than four hours a day! Sleep is meant to re-vitalise and re-energise us and some researchers have since expressed contrary opinion to that of Thatcher. Lack of good sleep is detrimental to health in the long run and we know this without any expert telling us and actually productivity may decline as a result!

So get enough sleep and I am not recommending the number of hours you sleep but you will know what works best for you. Bernard Hopkins is about 50 years of age and still boxing at the top level against 20 year old boxers; still beating top level young boxers. He doesn't make any secret of his regime and diet; he sleeps at 9.00pm every day and wakes up at 4.00am; that's 7 hours of sleep! Sleep scientists have concluded that the sleep before 12 could be counted as twice the hour because the body clock is designed to get the most benefit during those hours. You will know what works for you but productivity drops towards evening and instead of sitting behind the TV for three hours after dinner, it is good to get into bed early and you will have ample time to start your day early to get important things done before the distraction of the day starts. This is my own routine but you may be more alert in the night so do what works for you.

A simple step to getting a good sleep is to have a

routine and your body will adjust to it. Avoid alcohol and caffeine close to bedtime as these interferes with your sleep pattern and this is supported by empirical research data. Make your bedroom conducive with the right temperature, comfortable beddings and avoid clutter. Switch off all electronics before going to bed and clear your mind of the day's work. Get the best sleep and you will be re-energised for the day ahead.

During the day when your body slows down for a nap, don't deny it; just take a nap but make sure it is less than 30 minutes otherwise it may have counter-productive effect. Naps restore sensory perception and mental acuity and it is like a recharge of your battery in the middle of the day. I am a morning person and when I take a nap, I am restored to the energy and creativity I have in the early mornings and I use this for my creative work.

The next chapter looks at the other relevant and useful piece of advice to help boost your mental and physical energy thereby helping you become more efficient as well as increasing your productivity.

You may think that you will implement this as soon as you finish this book but trust me it takes discipline to change the way you have always worked and if you find yourself going back to your old ways after days of trying this, you are not alone! Let me give you a tip on how to kick-start this process, implement them gradually rather than trying to do it all at once; when you are accustomed to one of the points then move on to the next one. Another trick is to also revisit this topic again and again.

You must remember that time is given unto us equally and you have the same time as a billionaire or a president of a country, so treat your time as your most precious resource and make the most of it. When you lose money, you can regain it but when you lose time, it would never come back!

CHAPTER 20

Mental and Physical Energy

"The energy of the mind is the essence of life"
- Aristotle (384—322 B.C.E.,
Greek philosopher and scientist)

Whatever goal you have set for yourself including running a successful business can only be accomplished when you have the energy to get it done. Physical energy is derived from two sources literally; food and exercise. Remember the phrase *'You are what you eat'*? Yes, it is very true. I am not a nutritionist but I know that there are some kinds of food that provide energy and some foods that drain energy. You will know from your experience which food provides you with energy and the ones that deplete energy! Caffeine energy is short-term as it gives you a lift instantly, but the energy level plummets very quickly and you will be looking for the next fix!

My favourite breakfast is oat meal and it releases

energy slowly without giving you the lift/plummet sequence. I never liked oatmeal as a kid as it doesn't look appealing enough for me. One day I watched on TV a spritely 96-year-old being interviewed about the secret of his longevity, he said his favourite breakfast is oatmeal and he has been eating it for 80 years; I was hooked from that day. Please don't laugh at me! It doesn't matter whether that information is true or not but it is enough to change my choice of breakfast and I love it! Seriously, you need to learn a little bit about what food is good for you because it isn't the same for everyone.

Some people think that exercise would make them tired but that's not particularly true. Exercise energises me personally and I feel powerful and capable of achieving anything; even a day after exercise is even more productive because I have recovered and would be brimming with energy. Timothy Zachery "Timbaland" Mosley, the American rapper, record producer, and songwriter was at a time in his career, very fat and his career was dwindling, according to a TV program. He took charge of his life through exercise and the consequent weight loss. According to the MTV program, Timbaland's career took off again and he has never looked back. If you are tired and lethargic all day long even if you are not overweight, go running or hit the gym and see how quickly your mood changes. Talking about mood changes, it is all about your body and your mind. Have you heard the phrase '*A healthy body is a healthy mind*'? How do you achieve a healthy mind? Your mind is also like your body; you must feed it with positive ideas. The only difference and the most dangerous habit of the mind is that unlike your body which cannot feed itself except you put something in your mouth; your mind has a mind of its own and would feed itself non-stop whether you feed it or not! Yes, you can quote me on that.

Your mind doesn't understand the word idleness; it is restless and can be wild sometimes. Sometimes you might just be minding your own business and your mind would just go out there to find a scary picture for you to view; you will be wondering; where is that from? Have you experienced that before? Surely, except you are from Mars! The mind is not the boss but if you give it an inch, it would park a car. How do you tame this wild child called the mind? Just like a mischievous child, keep it busy, give it work to do, give it the direction to go and it would obey you most of the time; but you have to train it and get into the habit of positive thoughts. The mind is like a magnet and it constantly attracts thoughts of similar nature non-stop.

Do you know you can only hold a thought one at a time? So, if you find your mind wandering to a place you don't want, just change your thought to a positive one immediately. Anytime I encounter an unwanted thought, I have trained my mind to change to a picture of one of my goals and it works every time. Please don't go back to check if it is there or not because that's a reverse gear and it may spin you back into the unwanted thoughts. I love this quote by Kiran Aditham '*A mind is a terrible thing to waste but a wonderful thing to invest in.*' How do you invest in your mind? The energy of the body is food while the energy of the mind is the spoken or written words. When I say word, it includes pictures, music, art, movies etc. The quickest way to prime your mind for instantaneous change is through music especially the kind of music you love. The foundation of civilisation is the discovery of writing and mankind hasn't looked back since then. Great men are mostly regarded as such because of their minds; even sportsmen that rely on their physical prowess still need a great mind to succeed. I follow sports keenly as you must have noticed already in this book, so I would give you an example of someone with a great athletic body and you will be able to relate to my view of the importance of mind-set if you want to succeed at anything at all. If you, like me, follow athletics, you will know Asafa Powell, the Jamaican Athlete that broke the world record at a time it was thought impossible to go any lower than 9.79 set by Maurice Green since 1999.

The record stood for more than six years before Powell pummelled it down to 9.77 in 2005 at Athens. A new superstar is born, hailed many journalists. The feat of actually breaking any world record is phenomenon in its own right but to break a record in an event that's incredibly as difficult as 100m is even more sensational. Asafa Powell didn't stop at that but he did it again in 2007 reducing the record to 9.74 at Reiti. 1}People raised their expectation of Asafa Powell and many thought that is it, he is going to dominate the sport forever and that the record this time would never be broken! I stand to be corrected, I don't think there is any other athlete in history of the sport with two world records in 100m without an Olympic Gold Medal in the event! As at the time of writing this book, Asafa Powell's name is in the record book but he still hasn't won an Olympic Gold Medal in 100m! He does well at ordinary events, but when the chips are down at major competitions, something in his mind wavers and he just doesn't perform to expectation. The press harshly calls him the man for the small occasions. Success is all in the mind! How can I tell this story without talking about Usain Bolt, the current 100m world record holder as well as numerous gold medals too many to count! I would have loved to say he is the nemesis for Asafa Powell's fate but even before Bolt, others have beaten Powell in major competitions denying him of the coveted gold medal. Bolt is always happy or at least seems to be at the starting line-up and he gets it right most times except once where he false-started at the World Championship!

Sports, they say is 90% mental and 10% physical and so is life! I have read many discourses about the veracity of that phrase but in my opinion and in the context of our discussion here, I think I agree more than I disagree! Now let's come back to feeding your mind with positive thoughts! How do you do it consistently to create habit that would endure for the rest of your life? Read. I read a lot of biographies of great people because what they have written was derived from their thoughts and when you read their books, you also begin to think like them. Since we know that our thoughts translate to our lives, then we are most likely to emulate the habits of thoughts of these authors. Personal growth books are viewed with disdain by some people but my house is full of such books! I would confidently say that I am motivated to contribute my own thoughts to the genre simply by admiring the work of some of the authors. Oprah was reviewing a book on her program, *Super Soul Sunday* and she claims to have read mountains of self-help books and still she finds something new to learn from every book she reads! Why is Oprah still reading self-help books? She is apparently feeding her mind with positive thoughts because if you have cultivated the habit of inhabiting the positive space of light, you don't want to go back into darkness. If Oprah is still reading self-help books, I don't know if you have any excuse because she is one of the busiest people in the world. By the way, she is also one of the richest women in the world which tells you success doesn't happen by accident. Another favourite superstar I admire is Will Smith, he also reads a lot of personal growth books and I am not surprised at his meteoric rise as well as his staying power. One of Hollywood's busiest superstar remains on top after decades of success. There was a lot of press about his children saying profound things about quantum physics and the inadequacy of the school system; he obviously has infected his kids with the bug of rapacious learning desires.

Get rid of negative energy from your mind and replace it with positive energy. Unlike positive thoughts, which you have to cultivate, nurture, woo and cajole to attract, negative thoughts aren't that shy, they are ruthless, strong and bold. They are roaming looking for uninhabited mind to populate and the moment they find a seat, they quickly multiply themselves rapidly and you may find it difficult to get rid of them. What are the sources of negative thoughts that are very obvious from practical experience? Nelson Mandela once gave the analogy that hatred is like drinking poison and expecting your enemy to die! What?! I never thought of it that way and since that time I don't harbour hatred against anyone regardless of the thing they might have done.

"Man must evolve for all human conflicts a method which rejects revenge, aggression and retaliation. The foundation of such a method is love."
- Martin Luther King, Jr.

Align your mind and body into a state of unison embodied by positivity, purpose and love. If you do that, life becomes a bliss that it is meant to be!

CHAPTER 21

Change: The Opportunity to Grow

"It may be hard for an egg to turn into a bird: it would be a jolly sight harder for it to learn to fly while remaining an egg. We are like eggs at present. And you cannot go on indefinitely being just an ordinary, decent egg. We must be hatched or go bad..."
- CS Lewis (1998 – 1963, British novelist, poet, academic, medievalist, literary critic, essayist, lay theologian, broadcaster, lecturer, and Christian apologist, born in Belfast, Ireland

One of the greatest visionaries of our time in the business arena is Steve Job. He has subsequently amassed a massive number of admirers and I am one of them. He gave one of the best speeches at the Stanford Commencement in 2005 in which he talked about how he dropped out of college because he thought the money being paid by his parents cannot be justified by what he was being taught. He stayed around to attend those courses he loved albeit unofficially and when satisfied he had learned enough he left the college. Dropping out of college was the driving force of his life from my observation and if he hadn't dropped out, it is unlikely that he would have developed the burning desire to change the world which in a way he did!

His life was characterised by a tsunami-like change; he was kicked out of Apple the company he co-founded and he confessed that he was distraught. The sacking was not only humiliating but also cost him some of his life investment! He weathered the storm and came back to save Apple and took them to the top as the best company in the world.

Bill Gates – he is one of the richest men in the world and he needs no introduction. He also dropped out of Harvard to pursue his dream of writing software for a new product called Altair 8800; he felt if he waited to finish his degree other people might get the opportunity before him. The rest, as they say, is history.

Michael Dell - This is the guy behind the Dell Computers and he started this business whilst in school and was so successful he dropped out to fully grow the business into a multi-billion dollars company.

I have given you three familiar examples of change which cannot be taken lightly in the lives of these great men. Look around you and you will find your own examples of where a seemingly difficult change caused an individual to change his life for better and contribute to the world in the process.

Why are people so afraid of change? Most people are

afraid of making the wrong move which may lead to disaster and in their minds it is safer to remain static or stay the same. A bird in hand is worth 10 in the bush but as you hold on to your lonely bird other people are helping themselves to the 10 birds eager to be in someone's hand. The bird analogy here refers to opportunity and if you don't go out there and do something, there are chances that you will remain where you are; not only that, you will start to decline because life is in flow and it would not permit you to be in one place for too long. The earth rotates around other planets so that's evidence that the species in it are designed to move both physically, mentally and spiritually.

If you live in a particular street for years, you will notice that there must be movement, if you don't move other people are moving in and out of the street; that's the way it is meant to be! Life cannot be static and if we understand this principle it should encourage us to make a move, take a risk, change position; this is the only way to grow.

The butterfly is a beautiful creature and it flies with elegance and ease and we all admire it. You will hate to touch the creature just one step before becoming such a lovely creature. It is at the larva stage and it is not good to look at, let alone touch! This is nature showing us that life process is not static and that change is inevitable whether we like it or not. Babies are the most beautiful things in the world and the emotion they generate cannot be surpassed by anything else in the world! Before the baby becomes such a wonderful and beautiful thing we drool about, it was a foetus and if you see what a 4 week old foetus looks like; it isn't pretty at all. I shall now revert back to the quote by the thinker, CS Lewis:

"It may be hard for an egg to turn into a bird: it would be a jolly sight harder for it to learn to fly while remaining an egg. We are like eggs at present. And you cannot go on indefinitely being just an ordinary, decent egg. We must be hatched or go bad."

Can you imagine an egg flying? Nope! It has to hatch and become a bird, and then it has the permission to learn to fly. However, an egg cannot remain an egg for too long because it would go bad! You cannot remain the same, it is either you are moving forward or you are moving backwards: there is no middle-ground because life itself is in flow. So, you decide where the flow takes you. If you don't decide where the flow of life should take you, then it would take you anywhere it pleases! It is very unlikely that you fly but most definitely likely that you will be grounded and you will not even be grounded for too long before you go bad just like the egg! Change will happen to us whether we like it or not! From the time I started writing this book to this moment, I have experienced a lot of changes in my life and I have learned to embrace it and make lemonade out of a lemon and possibly find someone with vodka to share it with!

A lot of money has been spent exploring the idea that there could be water and therefore life on other planets;

some people think this is a waste of time and money but personally I think whatever the value of investment in this area, it cannot be too much and I salute the governments and companies engaged in this endeavour! When you pursue seemingly impossible goals, you may find bigger and better things along the route towards accomplishing your goals. Whether you accomplish your original goal or not is irrelevant, nature has a way of rewarding initiatives, it could be a direct reward or an indirect reward! It is a direct reward if you actually accomplish the goal in question or indirect reward by finding something else bigger in your quest towards achieving the original goal! Scientists stumbled on the popular drug Viagra while conducting experiments to invent a drug for pulmonary heart conditions. History is littered with the discovery of a completely different solution in the pursuit of a particular goal. This happens in everyday life and in my opinion; it is a reward for initiatives. The number one driver of initiative in our society is change, when your livelihood or life is threatened by an unexpected event; you need no motivation to drive towards your goals. This is why so many great things are done by those threatened by an enforced change rather than an initiated change!

Some people may associate change with adversity, they are right in a way because any change that is easily managed or handled are unlikely to move people to action and this is the reason why it is important that we embrace adversity as a gift! It might not seem like one at the time but in my own experience, every time I experience any serious change that I consider unwanted, in hindsight it always leads to something greater in my life.

There is no business if there is no change! Change is to business what water is to plant. If you don't like the heat get out of the kitchen; I would say if you don't like change get out of business! We know it's not all change that is good at least in the short-term but change would force you to do things differently and put fire under your pants such that you have no choice but to do more and be smarter in your approach.

When next you encounter change, even if it is a difficult one, grit your teeth and embrace it! This is a sure way to succeed in life and in business.

CHAPTER 22

Contribution

"Money has never made man happy, nor will it; there is nothing in its nature to produce happiness. The more of it one has, the more one wants"
- Benjamin Franklin (1706 – 1790 , renowned polymath, leading author, printer, political theorist, politician, postmaster, scientist, inventor, civic activist, statesman, diplomat and one of the founding fathers of the United States)

Think back to the big goals that you set a while back which has now been achieved. The euphoria may last for a few days or weeks, depending on how much you value the achievement. Henry Ford was once one of the richest men in the world and his view of wealth would amaze you. He thought that wealth is useless if not directed towards providing great service to the community. No matter how rich you are, it is impossible to sleep in two rooms at the same time or on two beds; well you may have two beds in your bedroom but you are still likely to sleep in one otherwise your family may call the doctors for help if you straddle between two beds! You cannot drive two cars at the same time. Ford concluded that pursuit of wealth for personal aggrandizement is pointless!

I totally agree with him. Human beings no matter the culture, location or race are always pursuing something, and rightly so otherwise life would be so boring. The common saying that life is too short is absolute rubbish, the reason why it seems so is that we are always pursuing something whether we know it or not. Let's do some imaginative exercise. Imagine that you have all the money in the world, whatever you want if you say it you get it. Anything at all. If you have nothing to look forward to, if everything comes to you when you want them; one year would seem like fifty years. It is unlikely that you will want to live up to twenty years, because it would be totally meaningless. Golf takes five hours or more to play and it was invented as a solution to the boredom felt by the rich people because they don't have to strive for a living and life was very frustrating for them despite their wealth! Golf helps a little bit but your mind can't stand doing the same thing over and over because it would habituate. Let me give you an example everyone can relate to; if you listen to a music you like for the first time, it feels wonderful. It is even better the second time and third time. By the time you listen to it 100th time, you are unlikely to get the same euphoric feeling as it was at the beginning. What I am trying to explain to you is that mankind thrives on challenges, something to conquer and something to look forward to!

Boxers live for belts and if you imagine what they put

themselves through to prepare for a fight, you will be amazed. As you well know now that I follow sports, so I observe human behaviour in addition to enjoying the games. A world title fight between a world champion and a challenger was cancelled because the world champion tested positive to a banned drug and the belt was awarded to the challenger. Now put yourself in the shoes of the challenger, if you have been preparing all your life for a single goal and you now have it on a platter, how happy would you be? It would surprise you that the challenger was very disappointed because he didn't feel that he earned the belt, he felt it was awarded to him and he was pushing for a fight like crazy to show the world that he truly deserves the belt. He got his wish, another world title fight with his belt on the line and he won fair and square. I have never seen anyone celebrate like that for winning anything. My point is that for us to feel validated, we must earn whatever comes to us.

I wasn't born with any silver spoon, not even a bronze spoon! Well, I am eternally grateful to my parents because they gave me first and foremost, love and then, education. Children don't usually realise that their parents aren't rich until they see a different reality from what they experience at home. If you are not poor, you cannot appreciate riches. I notice that some of my friends in school have some privileges that I didn't have and I started asking my parents questions about why can't I have this and that. They gave love and attention instead of material things and I was a happy child. As we grow older, I started to notice that my friends aren't as happy as I imagine they would be! I can't believe these kids have all these privileges and they are still unhappy. I was really precocious as a kid and always on top of my class and my parents were usually proud at the end of the year's parents/teachers gathering where the best students are called out and awarded gifts. My close friend with the rich parents would rather be like me! I thought that was bizarre! He confided this secret when we were much older. He didn't like it that he was getting everything that he wanted. He felt that I was doing better than him in school because I was more motivated to change my life but he couldn't find similar motivation because his life was comfortable already. I didn't even know what motivation was at the time and it wasn't that I did anything outside the classroom, it was just a gift! He interpreted it differently. Children of rich parents have it all to do because their greatest fear is that people may think that they are successful because of help from their parents! If you doubt this, I would tell you two stories to buttress the point.

Do you know the musician Julio Iglesias, his son Enrique had all the privileged upbringing anyone could have wished for and he secretly wants to be a musician. Enrique doesn't want his father to know about his plans for a music career and doesn't want his famous surname to help advance his career. He borrowed money from his family nanny and he recorded a demo cassette tape which consisted of a Spanish song and two English songs.

Approaching his father's former publicist, Fernand Martinez, the two promoted the songs under the stage name 'Enrique Martinez' with the backstory of being an unknown singer from Guatemala. Iglesias was signed on to Fonovisa Records. After dropping out of college, he travelled to Toronto to record his first album. Enrique Iglesias sold over 137million records and is one of the world's great artists! He is a very clever guy and he understands this principle at such a young age and it is likely he wouldn't have been as successful if he lives with the guilt that his father's name was the reason for his outstanding success. He doesn't need to prove it to anyone really, he only needs to prove it to himself and he is satisfied that he is a self-made musician and a millionaire to boot. Inherited money or privileges are much more difficult than creating your own wealth, when things are given to us without effort, our soul rejects it and the repercussions could be devastating. If you observe the society, you will see many examples like that of Enrique Iglesias, children of rich and famous determined not to get help from their parents to make their own way in life. Contrast this with the next story which you are all probably familiar with.

Whitney Houston as a singer was a legendary figure in the music industry and when you are that good and that famous, riches must follow. She was interviewed years ago about her wealth and she said it was just a normal life, all the material things are no longer exciting because you are used to it and it is your daily existence and to quote her she said:

"It becomes an alright life", which means it is ok but not as special a life as imagined by her teeming fans. You have seen the example of Enrique but it was impossible for Whitney's daughter (Bobbi Brown) to disguise herself and carve out a career without anyone noticing who she is! She doesn't have to go into music; she could have done anything else in life, it is likely the world would still feel it was not all down to her own effort. Nothing hurts more than putting every fibre of your soul into something and the credit is taken away from you. Bobbi's life has played out in public and when a kid has more money than she can spend in a lifetime it is a burden. She was not the first rich kid to have allegedly taken drugs and would not be the last, it was tough for them. As I write this page, Bobbi is still in a coma, kept on live support after being found in a bathroom tub just like her mother and the whole world has been praying for her. *(Bobbi Kristina Brown sadly passed on to the great beyond on Sunday 26th July 2015 aged 22).*

Why have I told you these two stories? If you are accumulating money and a lot of it to pass to your children, it is an exercise in futility! If that was your motivation up till now it is not too late, you can still switch your motivation to something else i.e. service to humanity! You will derive much more happiness making the world better than having untold riches passed on to your children and possibly burden them with guilt for the rest of their lives. Bill Gate was asked about passing his fortune to his children and the cleverest answer I have ever heard was *"I would leave enough money for my children to enable them do whatever they want to do but not enough for them to do nothing."* True to his words, he has set out to give his money away to rid the world of dangerous diseases and lift people out of poverty. Sometimes the universe favours some people because their intention is great from the outset. Warren Buffett is also committed to giving his fortunes away and has already passed on some of it to Bill Gate to pursue such a worthy agenda. These two men are giants in the history of the world but another great persona which established this principle of giving away fortunes is the man who inspired Napoleon Hill to write the book *'Think and Grow Rich'*, Andrew Carnegie. He was responsible for most libraries in the western world because he believed that education is the key to progress in this world. He also gave most of his fortunes away and his name is written in gold forever.

I want to show you that contribution is greater than personal wealth, and what I mean by contribution is not necessarily giving your money away which is not a bad idea either, but it is to show you that whatever you do that contributes to society, whether big or small, should be your primary motivation. Why? Henry Ford said when you think of service first and foremost, you cannot but attract money and this is the principle upon which he built a huge fortune. In our business and in our life, we should think first of the service we can render to benefit the society and do it. This is the path to the happiness that we have been seeking all our life. Money is not a bad thing but it is simply a means to an end and not an end in itself.

Would you decide today what worthwhile contribution you want to give back to the world? Your happiness and fulfilment is guaranteed and it doesn't have to be in the area of business. Find your own calling, find your own passion! Whatever you do, your driving force should be the desire to make contribution to the society

CHAPTER 23

The Gift of Crisis

My family members are in Nigeria and I speak to them regularly and sometimes when work pressures get too much we may not speak for a while. My two sisters are the best you can have in this world and they are both doing well in their various careers! My immediate sister was a warrior of a kind, she was simply fearless and she had conquered so many obstacles to succeed. She ran her own business and evidence of her success was obvious through the several properties that she owned. I would consider her the happy-go-lucky type, when you are with her you will laugh nonstop and she had a generous spirit.

Good people make wrong decisions sometimes as it turned out the man she married was with her for the money but it was obvious to everyone else, except my sister. She was allegedly badly treated and abused by this monster of a man and it wasn't a surprise to any of us. She was fed up with it and wanted to leave but somehow she was cajoled to stay and that was the biggest error of her life. On this day, I was coming back from work and my phone was in my laptop bag as usual. I have resorted to doing that since I lost a few mobile phones to pickpockets whilst using the London Underground.

   I brought out my phone on arrival at home and there were 37 missed calls on my phone! I knew straight away that something terrible must have happened. Was it my mum? I spoke to her a day before and she was hale and hearty, God please don't let it be my mum. It was at a time that when you want to make international calls you have to buy a phone card and then use the voucher number to make the calls. I literally ran to the nearest shop to buy the card and I called my mum, she answered and I was relieved! She was alright and I told her I would call her back soon. Then I called my sister Lola to check why everybody was calling me! She was in tears; Moji was shot by armed robbers while she was coming from the bank! I just froze! In Nigeria, armed robbers operate with impunity because the police are poorly paid, lack the necessary tools to fight crime and are corrupt! My encounter with armed robbers in Nigeria was quite a long time ago and it lasted just two minutes and it felt like two days. She was rushed to the hospital and the doctors managed to stop the bleeding but the bullet inside her was difficult to reach, so they decided to allow her to heal and the bullet would be removed later. I was speaking to her every day and she was in good spirit but very low on energy. One night, I promised to send her some money the next day, just something to lift her spirit. My mum was by her bedside throughout. It was a time when if you want to send money home you go to the agents and do money transfer, so I thought on my way from work I would go and transfer the money.

I didn't have to transfer the money eventually because as I was getting ready to go and do it; my other sister Lola called me about the death of my sister Moji! The world just stopped! How can this happen, but I still spoke to her yesterday! How?! Why?! As I write this I am really still very emotional though it was several years ago! So, the bullet inside her created a blood clot and that was sucked into her lung and she suffered heart attack at the hospital and shamefully they couldn't save her.

I was devastated because I have lost a confidant, a friend, a sister and nothing else in the world mattered at that point in time! So, that moment I spoke to her the previous day would be cherished for the rest of my life. I came home and told my wife and she just went to pieces. My children have never seen me cry but I cried for three days and didn't even get out of my bedroom. The third day, I realised that she is not coming back and I resolved to be there for his son and do something in her memory. I have dedicated this book to her loving memory among other things I have got to do.

How can you take a positive stance out of something so terrible? It helps me clarify the fact that, we don't have all the time in the world to do whatever we set out to do. Life is precious and we must cherish every moment of this wonderful experience. Abraham Lincoln said *"In the end, it's not the years in your life that count. It's the life in your years."* From that moment I stopped worrying about material things, I started thinking about what services I can render to the world so that I may make a difference. Since then I have done so many things including starting a business, a radio program teaching entrepreneurship and supporting a couple of charitable causes with my time and money. And the result of all these was simply down to the meaning I derived from losing someone so close and younger than me. It brought it closer home that whatever time we have got, we must not waste it on frivolous endeavours. Being happy is part of the commitment I have promised myself, being grateful for being alive alone is a great source of happiness for me!

So you have lost a bit of money, so what? You can make money anytime! You have lost in love? So what? That's your chance to find someone better! You have lost your job? That's your chance to become an employer! It is all in the meaning, it is all in the interpretation, when you give lousy meaning to an occurrence in your life, you get into a lousy state and you are probably paralysed with fear and unable to make rational positive decisions to make things better! Don't allow crisis go to waste! This is not philosophy or words to make you feel better; well what if it is words to make you feel better? When you feel better you are able to make good decisions. Let's look at some endeavours of men that generates pains.

Have you heard the saying by Francis Thompson that *"We were born in other's pain and perish in our own"*? I never gave it a second thought that for me to come into this world was quite a painful experience for someone; my mother that is! If you feel the pain women go through to have a baby, you will be more sympathetic when they are over-protective of their children. What nature is telling us here is that there can be no gain without some pain. The joy of a new baby is not comparable to anything in the world and I have experienced it three times so I am blessed. It is a case of so much pain and the aftermath is so much joy.

Without interfering with anyone's religion, I think there is probably incredible light of joy after death. Some people who have had near death experience have described the sense of overwhelming peace and light in the transition process! So after the pain of death there is light, peace and joy! So nature doesn't deviate from its established principles, when you feel pain remember this paragraph and make it so your interpretation is that of expectation of greater benefit than the pains.

So I have described to you the loss of my lovely sister in the most gruesome way not to mess with your day but to remind you that whatever happens to you in life, you can come out on the other side smiling. I coped with my loss by resolving to do something positive in her memory and also tell myself that life is a privilege; so I live everyday fully by enjoying the moment and doing something for the world that has given us so much. The dawn is the darkest hours of the night and yet the light is just very close by; when your pain seem the greatest, then your redemption is so close, don't lose it!

I work out regularly to keep fit, but I won't lie to you, sometimes you feel like, not today! So I muster the energy to go for it and I feel great after-wards. Your body produces endorphin after your exercise which is the feel good hormone. So, the pain of exercise leads to endorphin rewards. Muscles are built by breaking down the cells and healing it through the process of recovery. So when you build muscles you are stronger! So the process is Break-Heal-Strong! You cannot be strong in life without adversity and when you recognise this you will say, *'Bring it on!'* Never again would you be petrified of small pains. When you get small pains, you ask for bigger ones because you know the bigger the pain the better the rewards and the stronger you become, so you say, *'Bring it on!'* When life hits you on the head with a pebble, you ask for a brick because the bigger the pains, the bigger the rewards and the stronger you become, so you say, *'Bring it on!'* Let us stop running from the pains; let's embrace adversity, only then can we be stronger, better and richer in spirit and in life!

Business is exciting for one reason only, uncertainties! Business sometimes imitates life, if you play it safe in life you get average life; so it is in business too, those who go after the big stakes are those who win. He who dares win! It doesn't mean that if you go after the big stake you will win, you may not and that's the fun in it. If you are afraid of the future, afraid of adversity, you will not do a lot of things you are supposed to do; you limit what you do and this limits your opportunities to make a difference in the world. Stop thinking hopelessly about yourself, your small self, think about the world, what can you do for the world and if you encounter pains along the line, you will know that the reward is bigger than the pain. Do you want to be stronger, richer and happier? Embrace pain, embrace adversity.

Oprah Winfrey is one of the most admired people in the world and most people envy her successes but the making of the woman she is today is not without pains. When I say pains, it diminishes what she went through. So you want to be like Oprah, huh? Check this out; you will be sexually abused as a kid. You will be pregnant at 14 without any support from your parents. You will lose the child after giving birth. You will be betrayed by your mother. You will be physically abused by your parents….. All of this happening to you growing up as an innocent child! She makes no secret of her childhood hardship and challenges. By this singular act of openness, Oprah has saved so many lives, turned so many lives around and she is leaving a legacy of body of work that would be viewed with incredulity in hundreds of years' time! There are probably thousands of people with similar challenging tough childhood experience like Oprah but how many Oprahs do we have in this world today, very few! The difference between real Oprah who turns things around and thousands of people with similar experience but which were destroyed was simply one thing! That one thing is the interpretation they give their experience. Oprah thinks, well it is tough but I would pull through, do my best and use this experience to serve the world. Others feel life is unfair to them, wallow in self-pity and live a life of apathy. They may end up on the street, in jail or dead! What choice would you make with your experience? Oprah's choice or others choice? The choice remains strictly yours!

Steps to conquering crisis in whatever form it emanates

Identify the problem and don't make it bigger than it is! What meaning do you want to derive from it? Napoleon Hill said every adversity carries with it an equivalent advantage in one form or the other and you may not see it at the moment but you will connect the dot in future. Steve Job said in his valedictory speech at Stanford that dropping out of school paves the way for his humongous achievement in life and he could only connect the dot later in life that the universe is actually leading him towards his destiny. Nothing happens until something moves according to Albert Einstein so if there is anytime you need this principle it is when you are in crisis. So do something and move physically towards resolving the issues.

Build your strength physically by exercising and you will have enough energy to do whatever you need to do to confront the challenge. The good thing about exercise is that you also feel good afterwards; when in crisis, you must feel good otherwise you may be overwhelmed.

Build your strength mentally - read a book that proffers solution not necessarily to your current challenge but if you find one that does, that's great! Listen to motivational talks; there are millions of them on the internet. Talk to yourself positively constantly so that your mind will be filled with the energy to take the right step

Don't build up emotions within you - talk to someone you trust about your challenge. If you are the type that cry, don't hold it; cry if you have to: it is also a release but don't overdo it especially if it involves bereavement. When I lost my sister, I declared that I would mourn her for three days and after that I started thinking of what to do for her. In the case of a bereavement, it is an irreversible event and that is important to know and acknowledge; then the length of grieving is not a measure of the love you have for the person so do set a cut off line where you have to get on with life.

Ask for help! A lot of people are too proud to ask for help. It is not a sign of weakness! You will be amazed at how much help there is out there if you ask for it.

Focus on solution - spend less time worrying about the event but start focusing on the solution. Make a list of possible solutions and cross them out one by one as you explore and pursue them.

Build momentum - start with a solution that is easy to take action on and then move to more challenging ones; this helps you build momentum towards resolving the issues.

Ask the universe for guidance - it doesn't matter what your religion is, if you believe there is a higher power greater than you; then ask them to intervene! People of faith usually cope with life's adversity more effectively because they believe there is help coming from somewhere outside themselves, hence as a man thinks so is he!

Help others! This might sound counter-intuitive but it works like magic. When you reach out to help others when in crisis, you help yourself. I have seen this on many occasions where people that are in serious crisis go out of their way to help others and they manage to cope better with their own adversity. A young man in the UK was terminally ill having been diagnosed with cancer. Stephen Robert Sutton was focused on raising money for cancer charity and he appealed for help on *Facebook* and he raised over £4.96 million from over 340,000 donors, more than four times his target. He became an instant celebrity meeting the Prime Minister and other celebrities! This gave his life purpose and he achieved in his adversity as a teenager what 70-year-olds can only dream of.

Embrace challenges - you must cultivate a mind that embraces challenges and this is the biggest mental strength you could ever develop. When you are in this mode, you have bullet-proof attitude that would crush any challenge that comes your way!

Let me end this chapter with the words of the iconic President of the United States, JF Kennedy *"When written in Chinese the word crisis is composed of two characters; one represents danger the other represents opportunity."*

I would say to you, walk through the danger and grab your opportunity. Be fearless!

CHAPTER 24

Goal Setting

"Plans are only good intentions unless they immediately degenerate into hard work"
- Peter Drucker (1909 – 2005, the Austrian-born American management consultant, educator, and author. His writings contributed to the philosophical and practical foundations of the modern business corporation)

The world of business is littered with uncertainties and unexpected changes, it is a turbulent environment no matter where you live in the world. Why do you need to set goals when you don't have control over what is likely to happen in future, is it just a waste of time? I have referred to mind several times in this book and you will appreciate that I place great emphasis on it because it is key to our success in any endeavour that we embark upon in life.

Setting a goal focuses your mind towards the achievement of that goal. You must be deliberate in the use of your mind, if this is the only thing you take away from this book, it is more than enough! Your mind is constantly pursuing one goal or the other whether you set goals or not! How? Our brain cannot cope with the amount of data coming at us every second; if we pay attention to all of them at the same time, certain artery may burst as the workload will be impossible to manage! Therefore, our brain filters the data and pays attention to what is of interest to us and screens out the rest. Why our belief affects what we achieve in life is probably due to this system which is referred to as Reticular Activating System. Scientists have now found out that the system does more than regulate our arousal, sleep/wake transition; the system helps us pursue what we focus on.

So, if it is established that we have this system from a scientific viewpoint, how do we make the most of it in order to get what we want in life? This is the reason why setting goals is critical in the achievement of anything we want. If I put my mind to it, I can achieve it. I hear a lot of people say this and it is true; it is all a matter of focus! When you focus on something intently, your brain goes into action, gathering data similar to that which you focus on to deliver your solution. How you activate your brain to carry out this function is to ask questions and attempt to provide the answer(s). Do not worry if the answer doesn't come immediately because your brain will continue to look for the answer if you keep your focus on the question long enough.

Great inventors know this and this is why they are great. Thomas Edison who invented many of the great things we take for granted today had more than 1000 US patents but one of his greatest achievement was inventing the incandescent light bulb which is affordable to ordinary people to use in their homes. He had more than 10000 attempts before discovering the secret that brought light to the world literally. He didn't set a goal to just create a light bulb but one that is affordable to all and sundry. He focused on the goal and didn't waver until it was achieved.

Whatever goal you may set for yourself too could be achieved because there is a principle at work here, Edison was a genius no doubt but you have your own genius too and you even have better opportunities than him. According to the legend, he never stepped into any formal school but some critics disputed this and asserted he had three years of education! Whichever one is true is not important because even with three years of education if someone like him was capable of changing the world with his work, what excuse have we got? If you are reading this book you probably have more than three years of education, so you have better education than Thomas Edison but what are you doing with it? The principle he preached was that you pick one goal at a time and be persistent until the goal is achieved; this is total concentration of effort until the goal is achieved. Achieving this goal gives you confidence to set the next goal. Talking about confidence, I would like to talk about the importance of confidence in our life journey and some tips gathered from the masters in the field of psychology. We have now established that it is important to set goals in order to make progress in our business and life; the next step is how?

How Do You Set Goals

Decide on the goals you want to set and be specific - if your goal is about sales for the year, state the amount you intend to make during the year e.g. 200,000 dollars.

Break down you goals into small bite-size portions – In the words of Henry Ford: "Nothing is particularly hard if divided into small jobs." No matter how big your goal is, when you break it down into small tasks, psychologically, it becomes apparent that it is achievable and you are able to devote a little part of your time daily towards accomplishing them.

Discipline - Getting things done requires discipline and this is one of the most important ingredients in business and in life! Setting out an implementation plan and working hard to actually do the work involved is very critical. The trick is to learn to do small things quicker, you can then gradually move to doing bigger things quicker.

Emanuel James "Jim" Rohn (1930 – 2009) was an American entrepreneur, author and motivational speaker whose rags to riches story played a large part in his work and had tremendous influence in the field of personal development. This is his take on discipline:

"Discipline is the bridge between goals and accomplishment"

Implementation - Getting things done in business is more important than a well-crafted plan left in the drawer to gather dust! You must know your people well and give responsibility to those who are naturally inclined to get things done quickly. The thinkers are rarely doers but that's not a rule; it is just a guide so the important point is to delegate responsibilities to those who will get it done immediately. You can tell by what your people have done in the past. So set out your tasks, allocate responsibility, and decide the time-frame and review periodically to ensure actions have been completed properly.

Accountability - No matter how good your plan or implementation process is, you must hold someone accountable for the result and also reward excellence in a systematic way to send a signal to your team that good work shall be rewarded.

Review - Have you accomplished your goal? How would you know when you have done so? Measure your actual results against your plan and extract the difference! Investigate the disparity between your results and your plan with a view to addressing the reason for failure or inadequacy. When you have overachieved, look at your plan to see if you need to revise your plan upward for the future.

Goal setting will focus your mind on what you need to do to accomplish great things but more importantly you have a destination or end result in mind. You may then track back from that end result to where you are today and design your road map towards that goal.

CHAPTER 25

Confidence

"Optimism is the faith that leads to achievement. Nothing can be done without hope and confidence"
- Helen Keller (1880 –1968, American author, political activist, lecturer and the first deaf-blind person to earn a Bachelor of Arts degree)

How do you build confidence? Arsene Wenger, the manager of UK's Arsenal Football Club talks about building confidence slowly but you can lose it very quickly! I don't agree with him on that although I support his team. You can build confidence slowly and you can build it very quickly depending on your belief. Richard Bandler the founder of Neuro Linguistic Programming; who is the master in self-change management teaches that you can generate any emotion you want when you want it and this includes confidence. I would come back to the mind part of confidence but in the interim, let's review confidence in terms of how we use our body.

I have said it before and I would say it again that our body and our mind are intricately linked; so whatever emotion we feel is also reflected in our body. The human mind is trained to recognise through visual and physical cues when someone is confident or not. Do you need to be confident when you are eating your breakfast in the morning? Do you need to be confident when speaking to your children? General confidence level of individual differs from one person to the other and it doesn't matter what your level of confidence is at this particular moment; you only need to feel confident when the situation demands!

The opposite of confidence is anxiety and if we examine what causes anxiety, it is also different from one individual to the other; but basically this is caused by the need for us to perform! When we need to perform, confidence is very critical. There is always a mental component to every task we do; therefore we must train ourselves to feel the right kind of emotion when required. The body responds to stress or anxiety brought about by our perception of how good we think we are in performing the task at hand. The fear of embarrassment is at the centre of most anxiety. This is why public speaking is such a nightmare for some people to cope with because they are afraid of making a fool of themselves. There was a funny and cringe-worthy event lately involving a politician who completely froze in a bid to provide response to an analytical questioning by a journalist. And so the press had a field day making fun of the politician. Green Party Leader Natalie Bennett floundered woefully when asked about the cost of building the 500,000 housing units as contained in her party's manifesto. There are probably two reasons for the debacle; one could be lack of preparation or a lack of self-confidence or self-belief that she is competent enough to lead the party. It probably has nothing to do with her intrinsic ability as a leader but perhaps certain psychological subconscious self-talk!

Some brilliant individuals may make a fool of themselves not because of their intellect or lack of it but the inability to manage their emotions when they needed to! At the neurological level, if you feel you are not naturally a confident individual, you must eliminate this belief before you can cultivate a new competence of directing your emotion in the way that works for you. You must cultivate the ability to use the emotion you want when you want it.

There is a school of thought promoting the *'fake it until you make it'* syndrome; there may be a little truth in it, but I am not fully convinced of its long-term efficacy because it is difficult to live a lie for the long term, especially if it is a lie you are telling yourself constantly! The idea is that you pretend to be confident and after a while you will be! I have tested this with anger and it does work but not for very long. Sometimes as a leader, you have to employ some emotions when you need it to manage the performance of your staff. Sir Alex Ferguson is a master at using feigned anger to get his team to perform and by the evidence of his successes; you may argue whether this is a method worthy of emulation.

I am usually an unruffled character but I have

borrowed this method from Ferguson and it works like magic. I don't use it often except when standard is woefully unmet! In my experience, in the immediate aftermath of such encounter with my staff, I usually remain in that state of anger for a while until I learned to quickly remind myself that the anger is contrived; now I can return to my normal self and I usually end the episode internally with a laughter. So probably, there could be a little truth in the 'fake it until you make it' syndrome but I don't believe it works long term!

Physiological cues you may need to understand in order to use your body mechanisms to project confidence when you need to!

Breathing - Your breath is shallow and quick when anxious and one of the ways to deal with anxiety relating to performance is to breathe deeply and regularly counting from 10 to 1 or 1 to 10 depending on what works for you. Breathing deeply pumps oxygen into your brain and also helps you relax; so use it to calm down when you have to perform.

Body Posture – If you are not doing it, you would've seen or heard of parents admonishing their kids to stand straight and make their shoulders broader; this may cause you to feel bigger and confident especially when performing in front of an audience. Still on body posture, when next you watch a football match or any other games of great importance, study the body posture of the winning team at the end of the event and compare to that of the losing team. You will find that majority of the losing team members are exhausted, they may sit dejected on the pitch with the heads down, shoulders contracted, some walking slowly back to the dressing room. I once observed a team that had just lost in a penalty shootout. The player who took the last penalty kicked it over the bar and the team lost as a result. His head was down and he puts his hands on his head totally dejected. The captain accosted him pull him up, put his palm underneath his chin and raise it up literally and the player kept his head up and if you weren't told you wouldn't know that he's the one that just lost his team the game! Simple adjustment in the body posture of the player changes the outlook immediately. He is likely to still feel disappointed but his change of body posture changes the outlook at that particular time. Practice using your body to generate the emotions you want and you will soon become a master.

The use of emotion is a prerequisite for success in acting, and those who master this concept very well are usually on top of their game. Method acting, as you are probably aware, is a process where the actor takes on the total idiosyncrasies of the character for the period of scene or sometimes until the end of the day; some even take the character home with them. Can you practice method acting in little things and if you do it well, then you can generate any emotion you want anytime.

Charisma is defined as that rare personal quality of attractiveness or charm which inspires devotion from others! Grow your charisma by watching people said to have it and emulate what they do physically and mentally; it would not be long before people start describing you as such too. I believe anyone can learn anything if he is determined and focused enough.

Self-confidence is acceptance of yourself as you are. Most people are looking to change one thing about themselves that they don't like but it is all in our imagination. You are okay as you are because there is no other person exactly like you therefore you are a unique and rare individual - you are one in six billion hence you are not easy to come by. Inappropriate self-image is at the root of all insecurities and this is changeable if you want to. Sean Stephenson is my greatest inspiration when it comes to overcoming insecurities; this guy is 3ft tall and has been in a wheelchair since childhood. However, Sean has bullet proof confidence about himself and when he speaks; you are in awe of him! If anyone has any reason to feel insecure he has them in multiples but he refuses to allow physical attributes to define him! He says the body is just a container and no more; he also said we are an infinite being and we should be grateful for who we are! I share this philosophy of his and if you want to be inspired, search for his speeches on *YouTube* and you will never look at yourself the same way ever!

Mental Preparation - Most performers know that mental preparation is critical to their success and they leave no stone unturned in their pursuit of excellence. Prepare mentally when you have to perform any task well ahead of the time through rehearsal. This may be physical rehearsal as well as mental rehearsal. Imagine whatever you want to do going swimmingly well and visualise it so! I have explained about why doing new things makes people nervous sometimes; so the solution is to familiarise yourself with the event by visualisation, so that your brain will get used to the event and you are likely to be more confident in executing the performance.

Whatever you do in life, if you think you can you are right, if you think you can't you are also right; since confidence plays a great part in our success, we are better off growing it!

"All you need in this life is ignorance and confidence, and then success is sure." - Mark Twain

Mark Twain is talking about ignorance of your limitations, so don't take it literally. If you have confidence you are already on your way to success. The valedictory speech by Steve Job at Stanford also ended with something along the line of *"stay hungry stay foolish"* and I would add *"but be confident!"*

CHAPTER 26

Determination

Henry Ford said no one can stop a determined person from getting what he wants in life but he must be careful that in getting it, he is fair to the society from where he gets his desired goals. In life as in business, this ingredient doesn't rank very high in the personal development literature but I reckon it is as important, if not more important than other attributes like goal setting, confidence, beliefs etc.

Professional examinations are said to be notoriously difficult to pass, a notion that must not be believed because it isn't true. But what is true is that you must be prepared in order to pass. Before I even attempted any Accounting Professional Examination, I attended a seminar about the subject and it was delivered by one of the top professional accountants at the time. What he said resonated with me throughout my student days! This is an extract from the seminar, though not verbatim but it contained the substance of his message.

'*I am a precocious kid and I do not know what it feels like to come second and that is my standard. So when I write exams, engage in quizzes or debates I am usually the best; this is the pattern I maintain whatever I do in life. So I started my accounting professional examination with the same diligence and expectation that it's business as usual. I passed the entire diets one after the other and still don't even think anything of it except for people marvelling at my achievements! Then the final diet comes around and I expect to pass with ease as usual but that's not the case! So I think, not a big deal; there must have been a mistake somewhere. I would do it again and this time there would be no room for mistake either from me or from the examiner. Do it again, same bad result, do it again same bad result; six times before I finally reached my goal! When you get a knock on the head, again and again; you start doubting yourself and this is where determination comes in handy. A determined man may be afraid or in doubt but he would keep trying believing that something would show up. Unwavering determination is like a balloon pushed under the water it would find its way back up again and again!'*

He concludes by saying: *"I used to think I was brilliant until I failed my accounting professional exams six times in a row. When you start writing your professional exams, be prepared for it and be prepared to bounce back every-time you get a knock down. It may be at the beginning or at the end but remember my story and keep at it until you succeed."*

What is the worth of this story? More than 70% of those students who attended the seminar and listened to the story became Chartered Accountants a few years later because when someone you hold in high esteem confessed to you that he failed several times to get his goal, then when you stumble along the line you are likely to remember that you can always bounce back. The lesson I learned from the story stays with me until today;

Chapter 26: Determination

I have no fear about any endeavour I embark on because I know if I am determined enough I would get my goals.

We all have dreams. But in order to make dreams come into reality, it takes an awful lot of determination, dedication, self-discipline, and effort.

Jesse Owens' triumph at the 1936 Olympics with four gold medals was regarded as one of the most outstanding sporting achievements ever; despite the fact that the record was equalled by Carl Lewis at the 1984 Los Angeles Olympics boycotted by Soviet Union. Anyone who thinks this man's accomplishment was just talent and no more must think again because to win a single Olympic medal takes years of consistent hard work and determination. Today, any athlete with potentials are swarmed by sponsors falling over themselves to pay handsomely for endorsement deals; that helped the athletes concentrate solely on training for the event. In the days of Jesse Owen, there was nothing like that at all especially for a black man when there was still segregation of the blacks from whites! At a time where opportunities are limited for his race, Jesse Owens dream was alive and well! He was training and going to school as well as working part-time to support himself and his dreams.

Since the dawn of civilisation, it is getting tougher and tougher to be the best at anything as more and more people are chasing the same dream. This man is made of sterner stuff and he excelled where others wither through sheer determination to be the best at his vocation!

Germany at the time of his triumph was headed by Hitler and a country where a widespread racial belief system subsists that the blacks are less superior than they are. The burden of that misplaced prejudice alone is enough to dampen the spirit of Owens but not a chance! He went, he saw and conquered! It is like going into the lion's den and bringing out the lion dead! He won four unprecedented Olympics gold medals. Many who witnessed his triumph were amazed at the feat alone but it is like looking at the symptoms of an illness and ignoring the cause! The four gold medals were thought to have been won at a single competition! Yes, this is true as a matter of fact, but it wasn't in reality won there and then but over four years of waking up at 4.00am in the morning to train and then go to school then go to work etc. day after day.

The level of perseverance and determination required to get to such a lofty achievement can only be imagined. Owens himself was quoted as saying that he worked harder than most athletes of his time despite his natural talents. So, it is not enough to be talented, it must be accompanied by hard work and determination.

"Nothing in this world can take the place of persistence. Talent will not: nothing is more common than unsuccessful men with talent. Genius will not; unrewarded genius is almost a proverb. Education will not: the world is full of educated derelicts. Persistence and determination alone are omnipotent."

- Calvin Coolidge Jr. (1872 – 1933, the 30th President of the United States and a Republican lawyer who worked his way up the ladder of Massachusetts state politics, eventually becoming governor of that state).

Persistence and determination override talent any day as eloquently describe in the above quote from Coolidge. If you observe your society there are plenty of men with talents but without purpose; they remain unsuccessful except they embrace those twin words - persistence and determination. Determination will help you concentrate on the task at hand until it is accomplished and when you get bumped here and there, it would help you stay the course till success is achieved.

The journey from A to Z cannot be accomplished without obstacles. It is just like your normal road; regardless of how you travel, surely the journey is never smooth and straightforward. You will encounter street lights, pedestrian crossings, there are bumps on the road, traffic, other road users competing for space etc. When you embark on a journey and there is a bump on the road; it is unlikely that you will turn back and go home! This is what some people do when they encounter an obstacle in the process of chasing their dreams; they stop and turn back or just remain there! If you pass the bump and you see a busy traffic light intersection, would you turn around and go back? Not likely! So when you quit on your stool that's what you do!

Most people are good starters but not good finishers! Failure is actually evidence that you have tried something new! Some men don't even give themselves the chance to fail at something; they start an endeavour and they encounter a little obstacle and they throw in the towel; they are done, no more.

So your journey from *A* to *Z* is your goal; if you keep going when you encounter a bump, a traffic light, a zebra crossing or even an accident by the side; you will eventually get there! Give yourself a chance, arm yourself with unwavering determination and your goals are just within reach!

"Never go backward. Attempt, and do it with all your might. Determination is power."
- Charles Simmons (1893 – 1975, British lecturer, journalist and politician)

CHAPTER 27

The End is the Beginning

"Now this is not the end. It is not even the beginning of the end. But it is, perhaps, the end of the beginning."
- Sir Winston Churchill (1874 – 1965, British statesman and Prime Minister of the United Kingdom from 1940 -1945, and 1951 - 1955)

My goal in writing this book is to inspire you, the reader to pursue that idea of lifelong learning and if only one person takes this on and apply it then my job is done! I have read a lot of inspiring books in my life and I would not trade what I have learned through books or other means for a mountain of money or a pot of gold; it is worth much more than that! I know that I don't have all the answers and I don't have the privilege to tell you everything I know due to the constraints of space and time, but in the future you may see more work from me to address some of the issues still burning in my heart to share with the world.

Let's talk a little bit about hope because it is the string that holds the universe together and life would be meaningless without it. As you get on with your life after reading this book, I want you to go away with the hope that whatever happens in your life, there is a purpose for it and the change you desire can only come from you. Advancement begins with the man himself and you are responsible for the state of your life right now wherever you are on your journey of life.

The masters of today are the learners of yesterday, so when you decide that the change must start with you then you can move without hesitation to think, learn, do and achieve! Is it that easy? No! It is a journey and in reaching your destination there must be environmental influences that would force you to re-think, change, redirect, pause and continue moving until you reach your destination. When you think of life as a journey then you will realise that it isn't supposed to be smooth and once in a while bad things happen during the journey but your ultimate goal is to reach your destination. No matter how you travel there are so many things outside your control so embrace them instead of complaining about it or discouraged by it.

Road journey is full of its own difficulties like traffic lights, individuals driving under the influence (alcohol or drugs), heavy traffic, narrow bendy roads, redirection signs etc. Air travel has its turbulence, terrorism, bad weather, pilot errors, emergency landing etc. Travel by water is troubled by high winds, icebergs, pirates etc. You generally get the idea that no matter how you travel it may never be smooth and this is the same with the journey of life! The moment you realise that your destiny is in your hand, this is what would happen to you;

You will move from half-hearted approach to strength of purpose about any endeavour you lay your hands upon!

You will move from eye-service to self-motivation

You will move from seeing work as a chore to seeing every element of your work as fun!

In pursuit of any endeavour in life, there is this wrong notion that the higher you go the easier it becomes! Not a chance! The higher you go the more challenging it becomes! It is easier to get to the top than it is to remain there because other people as ambitious as you want to displace you! There is no life of ease at the top and life of ease is actually against the human psyche because you cannot stay in one place for too long; its either you are going forward or you will start slipping backward! Going up is slow and arduous but going back down could be very rapid indeed so when you get to the top which is very likely, then brace yourself for more challenges. Life of ease can only be synonymous with poverty or a state of apathy. When in a state of apathy, you don't care about anything including yourself and those in this state could become homeless or engage in self-destructive acts and their self-esteem is at the lowest. So, do you still want a life of ease? Those in a state of apathy could be described as having a life of ease because they don't need to exert mental or physical energy to do anything other than beg and live on others' pity! Surely, that's not the life you want.

So we must work and there is no substitute but in doing our work we must apply intelligence, we must be persistent and we must hope for a better tomorrow. If you have the hope that things would be better tomorrow you will do whatever it takes today to get to your goals. You must be certain that you will get the result you are after and this would give you the energy to walk through the brick walls to reach your goals.

> *"Learn from yesterday, live for today, hope for tomorrow. The important thing is not to stop questioning."*
> - Albert Einstein (1879 – 1955, German-born theoretical physicist who developed the general theory of relativity, one of the two pillars of modern physics)

How do you get to the truth? Einstein remains one of the most respected thinkers of his era and he admonishes that we must not stop questioning in his quote above. We have an enormous capacity to find answers to any questions we ask ourselves because our mind is designed to solve problems. One of the most astounding surprises to me is that we ask questions all the time but we usually ask the wrong type of questions about the wrong type of issues, especially the inconsequential ones. If we do know that our mind is capable of answering the questions that we ask, then we must learn to use this methodology and insight to solve significant challenges. The bigger your goals the more questions you must ask!

Chapter 27: The End is the Beginning

There are so many questions unanswered in our current era but some of the questions asked centuries ago have been answered by subsequent generations. For instance, lightning and thunder is nothing more than electricity but in certain cultures, a few people still regard the lightning phenomenon as mysterious and there is the god of lightning which is worshiped even up till today!

Benjamin Franklin questioned the phenomenon of lightning and he deciphered the mysterious scary lightning as just electricity! Albert Einstein questioned gravity and figured out the phenomenon and we all take the knowledge for granted today. What is your own truth? What is it that you are likely to find when you question your beliefs, desires and purpose? This is your assignment after reading this book.

The questions you ask yourself may lead you to the path of learning and therefore the path of knowledge and with knowledge you have everything, absolutely everything! Knowledge is power as they say and you have the advantage that you know how to apply the knowledge to get whatever you want in life as well as whatever you want for others!

We must accept finite disappointment, but never lose infinite hope.
Martin Luther King, Jr. (1929 – 1968, American Baptist minister, activist, humanitarian, and leader in the African-American Civil Rights Movement)

How can I talk about hope without reference to the symbol of hope; a man whose hope gave millions of blacks in US optimism at a time that instrument of states were used to maim, kill and suppress generations of black race in this country; a country which is now a symbol of freedom and self-appointed police of the free world! Martin Luther King's words still resonate with millions even many years after his death. He admonishes that we must never lose infinite hope! Infinite hope about our health, career, finances, emotions, relationships, freedom etc. infinite hope about the future; the hope that it shall be well in the end. Luther's dream of a fair and equal society was realised when President Obama was elected as the first black president of USA.

It's not *Eureka!* yet. There is a long way to go before his dream would be finally realised but a huge step was taken and it certainly would lead to other types of progress in the area of race relations. What is your hope and dream that would be realised in your lifetime and even after you have passed on? There is no way you can marvel at the achievements of President Obama without relating it to the dream of King!

Barrack Obama wrote the book, **The Audacity of Hope** years before becoming the President of the United States. The title is kind of intriguing to me and it gives you an insight into the mind of this great leader. His rise to greatness is one of this century's most daring effronteries to hope; considering his background, contacts, relative inexperience and not to be discounted,

Chapter 27: The End is the Beginning

his race! He has become an inspiration to millions of blacks and whites alike in US and around the world. You must hope that things will work out for you whatever your goal in life; without hope man will not even start anything! I have always been the one to hope that seemingly impossible dreams can be accomplished and as far I can remember this belief has always stayed with me. Let the hope that you are capable of greatness too go with you! It is a choice, you have no choice but to hope for greatness and you deserve it.

What I am saying here is that in whatever situation we find ourselves it is important to be hopeful that things would get better. If you don't hope, you will not even try so I want this to be my parting gift to you. Before I go, I want to introduce someone with the courage of a lion and the undying hope that he is capable of making a difference in his country. This man used to be in the Nigerian Army and fought in the Nigerian civil war; one of the worst tragedies a nation could experience and it was brutal as millions lost their lives! In 1983 when the irresponsible civilian government turned Nigeria into a state of anarchy, after recklessly rigging the election by stealing the people's mandate with the complicity of the judiciary. This man risked his life to sack the corrupt and inept civilian government to restore hope and decency to the image of the country.

He took over the reins of governance and within a short period of time, Nigerians are happy and could raise their heads again in the comity of nations. This singular act is enough and worthy of accolades but that's not the reason for bringing him into the picture here! I brought him here as a symbol of hope and you will see why in a moment! A few months into his reign as the Head of State of the Republic of Nigeria; some self-serving politically astute group of soldiers led by Gen Babangida took over the government in a bloodless coup defat! The only thing honourable about that act was not killing Gen Muhammadu Buhari, who as at the time of writing this book was just elected by Nigerians to replace Dr. Jonathan Goodluck; whose six years in the office was characterised by high-level corruption and infrastructural decay across the board.

Why is he a symbol of hope? Well, this was his fourth attempt at becoming the President of the country and at each attempt, corruption and massive election rigging prevented him from winning. But this dogged fighter is a true hero and he kept his hope of changing Nigeria alive until providence said enough is enough! Many people in his shoes would have retired to their village and live the rest of their lives in comfort. President Muhammadu Buhari was 72 years when elected and there is a great level of hope among Nigerians that this man would try his best despite the burden of old age.

He has transmitted that spirit of hope to millions of Nigerians and it is expected that he would make a difference and more importantly we can take a leaf from his purposefulness, determination and hope! I hope this book gives you the hope that whatever you hope to achieve in life is possible if only you can muster enough energy to hope!

"Three grand essentials to happiness in this life are something to do, something to love, and something to hope for."
- Joseph Addison (1672 – 1719; English essayist, poet, playwright, and politician)

THE END

About the Author

Ayo Benson trained as a Chartered Accountant; he is a Fellow of Association of Certified Chartered Accountants (ACCA) and he also holds an MBA from Oxford in United Kingdom. He is an Entrepreneur and Business Adviser for businesses. He has achieved a great deal in business with interest in e-commerce, media and publishing.

Benson has a radio program *'Goldmine of Your Mind'* where he teaches entrepreneurship in a unique, profoundly interesting and interactive format. He organises seminars and workshops to train entrepreneurship and personal growth. He is the founder of *Mannastores*, a procurement and logistics company based in UK and Nigeria, among other ecommerce businesses.

Benson has been interviewed by both the national and international media as a subject matter expert. He writes occasionally for some newspapers on business, personal growth and politics. Ayo Benson Olarewaju is a savvy social media expert with a commanding presence on *Facebook*, *Twitter* and *LinkedIn* amongst others. He also created the blog www.mannamart.blogspot.com with more than one million page-views.

Benson is a football lover and supports Arsenal Football Club of London